PENGUIN BOOKS

Huis Clos and Other Plays

The founder of French existentialism, Jean-Paul Sartre (1905–80) has had a great influence on many areas of modern thought. A writer of prodigious brilliance and originality, Sartre worked in many different genres. As a philosopher, a novelist, a dramatist, a biographer, a cultural critic and a political journalist, Sartre explored the meaning of human freedom in a century overshadowed by total war.

Born in Paris, Sartre studied philosophy and psychology at the École Normale Supérieure, where he established a life-long intellectual partnership with Simone de Beauvoir. He subsequently taught philosophy in Le Havre and in Paris. His early masterpiece, *La Nausée* (1938), explored the themes of solitude and absurdity. A remarkable collection of short stories, *Le Mur* (1939), further established his literary reputation. Conscripted into the French Army in 1939, Sartre was captured in June 1940 and imprisoned in Stalag XIID in Trier. He soon escaped to Paris where he played an active role in the Resistance. This experience of defeat and imprisonment, escape and revolt served to push Sartre beyond the flamboyant anarchist individualism of his early writings. *L'Être et le néant* (1943) is an elaborate meditation on the possibility of freedom. *Les Chemins de la liberté* (1945–49) is a trilogy of novels about the collective experience of war. In 1944 Sartre abandoned his careeer as a philosophy teacher. He was soon installed at the centre of Parisian intellectual life: editing *Les Temps modernes*, a literary-political review, travelling the world, quarrelling with Albert Camus, his erstwhile friend, and vigorously defending the idea of the Soviet Union against its Cold-War enemies. From 1944 until 1970, when his eyesight began to fail, Sartre enjoyed an immense international reputation as the most gifted, the most versatile and the most outspoken literary intellectual of the age. In a gesture that perfectly symbolized his audacity, he refused the Nobel Prize for Literature in 1964. Fired by a passion for freedom and justice, loved and hated in his own day, Sartre stands as the authentic modern successor to Voltaire, Victor Hugo and Émile Zola.

Jean-Paul Sartre

HUIS CLOS
and Other Plays

THE RESPECTABLE PROSTITUTE

LUCIFER AND THE LORD

HUIS CLOS

PENGUIN BOOKS

IN ASSOCIATION WITH HAMISH HAMILTON

PENGUIN BOOKS

Published by the Penguin Group
Penguin Books Ltd, 80 Strand, London WC2R 0RL, England
Penguin Putnam Inc., 375 Hudson Street, New York, New York 10014, USA
Penguin Books Australia Ltd, Ringwood, Victoria, Australia
Penguin Books Canada Ltd, 10 Alcorn Avenue, Toronto, Ontario, Canada M4V 3B2
Penguin Books India (P) Ltd, 11 Community Centre, Panchsheel Park, New Delhi – 110 017, India
Penguin Books (NZ) Ltd, Cnr Rosedale and Airborne Roads, Albany, Auckland, New Zealand
Penguin Books (South Africa) (Pty) Ltd, 24 Sturdee Avenue, Rosebank 2196 South Africa

Penguin Books Ltd, Registered Offices: 80 Strand, London WC2R 0RL, England

www.penguin.com

La Putain respectueuse first published by Gallimard 1946
This translation first published by Hamish Hamilton 1949

La Diable et le bon Dieu first published by Gallimard 1951
This translation first published by Hamish Hamilton 1952

Huis Clos first published 1944
This translation first published by Hamish Hamilton 1946

The first two plays published together in Penguin Books 1965
In Camera published in Penguin Books 1958
This collection published in Penguin Books 1982
Reprinted under the title *In Camera and Other Plays* 1990
Reprinted in Penguin Classics under the current title 2000
014

Printed in England by Clays Ltd, St Ives plc

CONTENTS

THE RESPECTABLE PROSTITUTE

CHARACTERS

LIZZIE
THE NEGRO
FRED
JOHN
JAMES
THE SENATOR
TOWNSPEOPLE

SCENE ONE

A room in a town in the Deep South. White walls. A divan bed. At right, a window, at left, a door leading to the bathroom. At back, a little anteroom leading to the front door. Before the curtain rises, a sound as of a storm on the stage. When the curtain rises, LIZZIE *is alone, in a skirt and blouse, using a vacuum-cleaner. The doorbell rings. She hesitates, looks towards the bathroom door. The bell rings again. She stops the Hoover and going to the bathroom door, opens it a little way.*

LIZZIE [*softly*]: There's someone at the door. Don't come out. [*She opens the door.* THE NEGRO *appears framed in the doorway. He is very tall and fat with white hair. He stands very stiffly.*] What is it? You've come to the wrong door. [*Pause*] Well, what do you want? Can't you speak?

THE NEGRO [*supplicating*]: Please, mam, please, mam.

LIZZIE: Please, what? [*She looks at him more closely.*] Just a minute. Weren't you in the train? You managed to escape? How did you find my address?

THE NEGRO: I looked for it, mam. I looked for it everywhere. [*He takes a step forward.*] Please, mam.

LIZZIE: Don't come in. There's someone here. What do you want?

THE NEGRO: Nothin'.

LIZZIE: What is it? What is it? Do you want money?

THE NEGRO [*pause*]: Please, mam, tell him I didn't do nothin'.

LIZZIE: Tell who?

THE NEGRO: The judge. Tell him, mam. Please, mam, tell the judge.

LIZZIE: Look, I shan't tell him anything. I've got enough troubles of my own, without getting mixed up in other people's. Now go away.

THE NEGRO: You know I didn't do nothin'.

LIZZIE: Sure, you didn't do anything. But I ain't going to no judge. Judges and cops, they give me the bellyache.

THE NEGRO: I got a wife and kids. ... I been walking all night. I can't go no further.

LIZZIE: Get out of town.

THE NEGRO: They'se watching the railroads.

LIZZIE: Who's watching?

THE NEGRO: The white folk.

LIZZIE: What white folk?

THE NEGRO: All the white folk. You ain't been out this mornin'?

LIZZIE: No. I haven't.

THE NEGRO: The streets is all full of people. Young folk and old folk; all talking together.

LIZZIE: How d'you mean?

THE NEGRO: That means I'se just got to run round and round till they catches me. When white folk start talking to strangers, some black man gonna die. [*Pause*] Tell them I didn't do nothin', mam. Tell the judge. Tell the newspaper boys. Maybe they'll print what you say. Tell them, mam, tell them, tell them!

LIZZIE: Don't shout. I tell you there's someone here. [*Pause*] Tell the papers – not on your life. I don't want any publicity right now. [*Pause*] If they call me as a witness, I promise to tell the truth.

THE NEGRO: You'll tell them I didn't do nothin'?

LIZZIE: I'll tell them.

THE NEGRO: Swear you'll tell them, mam?

LIZZIE: Yes, yes.

THE NEGRO: Swear by the Lord, you'll tell them?

LIZZIE: Oh, go to hell! I've told you I will, that's enough. [*Pause*] Get out!

THE NEGRO [*suddenly*]: Please, mam, hide me.

LIZZIE: Hide you?

THE NEGRO: Won't you, please?

LIZZIE: Hide you! Me? That's too much. [*She slams the door in his face.*] Gee, I've got enough troubles. [*She turns to the bathroom.*] You can come out now.

[FRED *comes out of the bathroom in his shirt-sleeves, without collar or tie.*]

FRED: Who was that?

LIZZIE: No one.

FRED: I thought it was the police.

LIZZIE: Police? Hey, are you in trouble with the police?

FRED: Me? No. But I thought you might be.

LIZZIE [*offended*]: I like that. I've never stolen a cent from anyone!

FRED: You've never been in trouble with the police?

LIZZIE: Not for stealing, anyway. [*She gets busy with the Hoover. The noise is deafening.*]

FRED [*annoyed by the noise*]: Hey!

LIZZIE [*shouting to make herself heard*]: What is it, sweetheart?

FRED [*shouting*]: You're deafening me.

LIZZIE [*shouting*]: Nearly finished. [*Pause*] I'm like that.

FRED [*shouting*]: What?

LIZZIE [*shouting*]: I say I'm like that.

FRED [*shouting*]: Like what?

LIZZIE [*shouting*]: Like that. The next morning I just have to take a bath and Hoover the carpet. [*She turns it off.*]

FRED [*pointing to the bed*]: While you're at it, cover that up.

LIZZIE: What?

FRED: The bed. I said cover it up. It stinks of sin.

LIZZIE: Sin? Where did you learn that word? You're not a preacher, are you?

FRED: No. Why?

LIZZIE: You talk like one. [*She looks at him.*] No, you're no preacher; you're much too clean. Let me see your ring. [*With admiration*] Boy, oh boy! Are you rich?

FRED: Yes.

LIZZIE: Very rich?

FRED: Very.

LIZZIE: That's fine. [*She puts her arms round his neck and offers him her lips.*] I think it's much better for a man to be rich. It inspires confidence.

[*He doesn't kiss her, and after a moment turns away.*]

FRED: Cover the bed.

LIZZIE: Okay! Okay! I'll cover it up. [*She covers the bed, and suddenly begins to laugh.*] 'Stinks of sin.' I'd never have thought of that. You know, boy, it's *your* sin. [*Fred makes a movement.*] Yes, I know, mine too. But I've had so many sins on my conscience ... [*She sits down on the bed and makes* FRED *sit beside her.*] Come here. Come and sit down. Don't look away. Do I scare you? [FRED *suddenly catches her brutally to him.*] You're hurting me! You're hurting me! [*He lets her go.*] Gee, you're a funny boy! [*Pause*] Hey, what's your name? Come on! I don't like not knowing your name. They hardly ever tell me their last names, and I can understand that. But their first names! How do you think I'm to tell one from the other if I don't know your names? Come on, sweetheart.

FRED: No.

LIZZIE: Okay, you'll be the one without a name. [*She gets up.*] Wait. I'm going to finish doing the room. [*She moves a few pieces of furniture.*] There. There. Everything tidy again. The chairs round the table – that always looks classy. Say, do you know where I can find a picture store? I want to buy some pictures. I got one in my box, a beauty. It's called 'The Broken Pitcher'. It's a picture of a little girl, and her pitcher is broken, poor thing. It's French.

FRED: What pitcher?

LIZZIE: I don't know: her pitcher. I guess she had a pitcher. I'd like a picture of an old grandmother to go opposite her. An old grandmother knitting, or telling stories to her grandchildren. Ah! I'm going to pull the blinds and open the window. [*She does so.*] Oh, what a beautiful morning! A whole new day beginning. [*She stretches.*] Gee! I feel wonderful; it's a glorious morning, I've had a grand bath, and I made love beautifully last night: I feel fine. I feel real fine! Come and see my view. Come and look. I've got a swell view. Ain't I lucky; my very first day and I found a room in the ritzy part of town. Ain't you coming? Don't you like looking at your town?

FRED: Yeah, from my own window.

LIZZIE [*suddenly*]: It ain't bad luck, is it, if the first person you see in the morning is a Negro?

FRED: Why?

LIZZIE: I ... I can see one on the sidewalk.

FRED: It's always bad luck to see niggers. Niggers are the devil. [*Pause*] Shut the window.

LIZZIE: Don't you want me to air the room?

FRED: I told you to shut the window. Right. And pull the blind. Turn the lights on.

LIZZIE: Why? Because of the Negroes? It's real nice in the sunlight.

FRED: No sunlight in here. I want your room to stay as it was last night. Now, shut the window, I said. I can get all the sunlight I want outside. [*He gets up, goes to her and looks at her.*]

LIZZIE [*vaguely troubled*]: What's the matter?

FRED: Nothing. Give me my tie.

LIZZIE: Okay; it's in the bathroom. [*She goes out.* FRED *quickly opens the drawers of the table and goes through them.* LIZZIE *comes back with the tie.*] Here it is! Come and I'll put it on for you. There. [*She ties it for him.*] You know, I don't like casual trade much, it means too many new faces. I'd like to settle down with three or four regulars, one for Tuesdays, one for Thursdays, and one for the week-end. I'm just telling you that. You're a bit young, but you're the serious type, and you might like the idea. Oh, I'm not saying any more. You can think about it. There! There! Gee, you're good-looking. Kiss me, handsome, kiss me. [*He kisses her roughly and then pushes her away.*] Oh!

FRED: You're the devil.

LIZZIE: Still talking like a preacher. What's the matter with you?

FRED: Nothing. I'm sick of myself.

LIZZIE: You got funny ways of showing it. [*Pause*] Are you pleased?

FRED: Pleased with what?

LIZZIE [*imitating him, smiling*]: Pleased with what? What a silly little girl you are.

FRED: Oh. Oh yes ... very pleased. Very pleased. How much do you want?

LIZZIE: Who's talking of money? I asked you if you were pleased, you might answer politely. What's the matter? Didn't you like me? Don't say you didn't like me?

FRED: Shut up.

LIZZIE: You took me in your arms and held me hard. And then very softly you said you loved me.

FRED: You were tight.

LIZZIE: No, I was not tight.

FRED: I say you were tight.

LIZZIE: I tell you I was not.

FRED: Well, I was. I don't remember anything.

LIZZIE: What a pity. I undressed in the bathroom, and when I came back, you blushed. Don't you remember? Don't you remember that I called you my little lobster? You turned out the light and made love to me in the dark. I thought that was very nice and respectable. Don't you remember?

FRED: No.

LIZZIE: And when we pretended we were two new-born babies in the same cradle? You remember that?

FRED: I told you to shut up. What a man does at night, belongs to the night. In the morning, you don't talk about it.

LIZZIE [*defiantly*]: And if I like talking about it? I enjoyed myself a lot, you know.

FRED: Oh, so you enjoyed yourself! [*He goes up to her, caresses her shoulders gently and then closes his hands round her neck.*] Do you always enjoy yourself when you think you've fooled a man? [*Pause*] I've forgotten last night. Completely forgotten it. I remember the nightclub, that's all. After that, you're the only one who remembers. The only one. [*He squeezes her neck.*]

LIZZIE: What are you doing?

FRED: I'm squeezing your throat.

LIZZIE: You're hurting me.

FRED: The only one. If I squeeze a little harder, there'll be no one left in the world who remembers last night. [*He lets her go.*] How much do you want?

LIZZIE: If you've forgotten, it's because I wasn't very good. I don't want to be paid for something that wasn't very good.

FRED: Stop jawing. How much?

LIZZIE: Listen. I only got into town the day before yesterday. You were my first customer. I won't charge the first one, for luck.

FRED: I guess I don't need your presents. [*He lays a ten-dollar bill on the table.*]

LIZZIE: I don't want your money, but I'm going to see what you think I'm worth. Wait, let me guess! [*She takes the note and closes her eyes.*] Forty bucks? No. That's too much, and there would be two bills. Twenty bucks? More? Then it must be more than forty bucks. Fifty? A hundred? [*All this while,* FRED *watches her, laughing silently.*] Oh well, I'll open my eyes. [*She looks at the note.*] Sure you didn't make a mistake?

FRED: I don't think so.

LIZZIE: You know what you've given me?

FRED: Yes.

LIZZIE: Take it back. Take it back at once. [*He refuses with a gesture.*] Ten dollars! Ten dollars! A girl like me, for ten dollars! I'll see you in hell first. You've seen my legs? [*She shows them.*] And my breasts, you've seen them? Are they ten-dollar breasts? Take your dirty money and get the hell out of here before I lose my temper. Ten dollars! You kissed me all over, you kept wanting to start all over again, you wanted me to tell you my life-story; and this morning, you were bad tempered, you bossed me around as if you'd paid for a whole month; and all that for how much? Not forty, not thirty, not even twenty; for *ten* dollars.

FRED: Yeah, quite enough too, for a slut.

LIZZIE: Slut! Slut! What are you, I'd like to know? What kind of a mother have you got, that she didn't teach you to respect a woman?

FRED: Shut your mouth!

LIZZIE: Son of a bitch! You son of a bitch!

FRED [*in an unnaturally calm voice*]: Listen, my girl! Don't talk to our boys too much about their mothers, or you'll get your neck wrung.

LIZZIE [*rushing up to him*]: Okay! Go ahead!

FRED [*backing away*]: Oh, shut up. [LIZZIE *picks up a vase from the table with the evident intention of braining him.*] Here's another ten dollars, but shut up. Shut up, or I'll have you put in jail.

LIZZIE: You'll have me locked up?

FRED: I will.

LIZZIE: You will?

FRED: I will.

LIZZIE: Don't give me that!

FRED [*violently*]: I'm Wilson Clarke's son.

LIZZIE: Who?

FRED: Senator Clarke's son.

LIZZIE: Yeah! And I'm Truman's daughter.

FRED: You've seen pictures of the Senator in the papers?

LIZZIE: So what?

FRED: Look here. [*He shows her a photo.*] I'm standing beside him, he's got his hand on my shoulder.

LIZZIE [*suddenly calm*]: Say! That your old man? Say!

[FRED *snatches the picture from her.*]

FRED: That's enough.

LIZZIE: Ain't he good-looking, though? He looks so good, so wise! [FRED *doesn't reply.*] Is that your garden?

FRED: Yes.

LIZZIE: And the little girls, are they your sisters? [*He doesn't reply.*] Your home's up on the hill?

FRED: Yes.

LIZZIE: So, in the morning, when you have breakfast, you can see the whole town from your window?

FRED: Yes.

LIZZIE: Do they ring a bell at meal-times to call you? You might tell me.

FRED: We have a gong.

LIZZIE [*ecstatically*]: A gong! I don't understand you. If I had a family like that, and a home like that, you'd have to pay me to sleep away from home. [*Pause*] I'm sorry I said that about your mother; I was mad. Is she in the picture, too?

FRED: I told you not to mention her.

LIZZIE: Okay, okay. [*Pause*] Can I ask you something? [*He doesn't reply.*] If you don't like making love, why did you come home with me? [*He doesn't reply. She sighs.*] Oh well! If you're going to stick around, I guess I'll have to get used to you.

[*Pause.* FRED *combs his hair in front of the glass.*]

FRED: You come from the North?

LIZZIE: Yes.

FRED: From New York?

LIZZIE: What's that to you?

FRED: You talked about New York last night.

LIZZIE: Anyone can talk about New York. That doesn't prove a thing.

FRED: Why didn't you stay there?

LIZZIE: I was sick of the place.

FRED: In trouble?

LIZZIE: Naturally. Trouble always comes to me, some people are like that. See this snake? [*She shows him a bracelet.*] It's his fault. He's my jinx.

FRED: Why do you wear it?

LIZZIE: As long as I've got it, I must wear it. They say the bad luck snakes bring is real bad.

FRED: Are you the girl the nigger tried to rape?

LIZZIE: What?

FRED: You got here yesterday morning on the six o'clock express?

LIZZIE: Uh-huh.

FRED: Then it was you.

LIZZIE: No one tried to rape me. [*She laughs a little bitterly.*] Rape me! See what I mean?

FRED: It was you. Webster told me last night, at the club.

LIZZIE [*pause*]: So that's it. That's why your eyes were shining so. It excited you, eh? With such a good father, too.

FRED [*pause*]: If I really thought you'd slept with a nigger ...

LIZZIE: Well?

FRED: I've got five coloured servants. When there's a call for me and one of them picks up the telephone, he wipes it before handing it to me.

LIZZIE [*with an admiring whistle*]: Gee!

FRED [*softly*]: We don't like niggers much here. Nor white girls who play around with them.

LIZZIE: That's all right. I've got nothing against them, but I wouldn't like them to touch me.

FRED: How do I know? You're the devil. Niggers are the devil too ... [*Abruptly*] So? He tried to rape you?

LIZZIE: What's it got to do with you?

FRED: Two of them got into your compartment. After a little while they attacked you. You called for help and some white men came to help you. One of the Negroes pulled out a razor and a white man shot him with a revolver. The other nigger got away ... Was that what happened?

LIZZIE: Of course it wasn't. The two Negroes were sitting perfectly still, talking together; they didn't even look at me. Then, four white boys got in, and two of them made a pass at me. They'd just won a football game, and they were tight. They said the place stank of niggers, and they wanted to throw them out of the window. The coloured boys did their best to defend themselves, and finally one of the white boys got a sock in the eye. Then he pulled a gun and fired. That's all. The other Negro jumped off the train as we got into the station.

FRED: We know him. He won't lose anything by waiting. [*Pause*] Is that what you're going to say when you come up before the judge?

LIZZIE: But what's it got to do with you?

FRED: Answer me.

LIZZIE: I ain't going to no judge. I tell you I hate trouble.

FRED: All the same, you'll have to go.

LIZZIE: I won't. I don't want anything to do with the cops.

FRED: They'll come and get you.

LIZZIE: Then I'll tell them what I saw.

FRED: You realize what you'll be doing?

LIZZIE: Doing?

FRED: You'll be defending a black man against a white.

LIZZIE: But the white man is guilty.

FRED: He isn't guilty.

LIZZIE: He shot a man, of course he's guilty.

FRED: Guilty of what?

LIZZIE: Of murder!

FRED: He only shot a nigger.

LIZZIE: Well?

FRED: If one is guilty of murder every time one kills a nigger...

LIZZIE: He had no right.

FRED: What right?

LIZZIE: He had no right.

FRED: That's just Yankee talk. [*Pause*] Guilty or no, you can't condemn a boy like him.

LIZZIE: Look, I don't want to condemn anyone. If they ask me what I saw, I'll tell them.

[FRED *marches up to her.*]

FRED: What's between you and this nigger? Why are you trying to protect him?

LIZZIE: I don't even know him.

FRED: Well then?

LIZZIE: I must tell the truth!

FRED: The truth? A ten-dollar whore must tell the truth! There is no truth; there are white men and black men and that's all. Seventeen thousand whites, twenty thousand blacks. This isn't New York; we have no right to fool around. [*Pause*] Tom is my cousin.

LIZZIE: Who?

FRED: Tom. The guy with the gun. He's my cousin.

LIZZIE [*understanding*]: Oh!

FRED: He comes of a very good family. Maybe that doesn't mean much to you; but he comes of a very good family.

LIZZIE: A man who comes of a very good family; who pressed himself against me and tried to lift my skirts. I can do without that sort of good family! I'm not at all surprised to find you're related.

FRED [*raising his hand, then restrains himself*]: You're a devil. You make a devil of everyone you meet.

LIZZIE: Let me go.

FRED: He made a pass at you – he shot a nigger – what does it matter? Those are things one does without thinking, they don't count. Tom is a born leader, that's what matters ...

LIZZIE: Maybe. But the Negro hadn't done nothing.

FRED: A nigger has always done something.

LIZZIE: I ain't giving no man away to no cops.

FRED: It's Tom or the nigger; you've got to sacrifice one. It's up to you to choose.

LIZZIE: So that's it. I'm up to the neck in it this time, and no mistake. [*To her bracelet*] Bloody jinx, this is what you do to me all the time! [*She takes it off and throws it on the bed.*]

FRED: How much do you want?

LIZZIE: I don't want a cent.

FRED: Five hundred dollars.

LIZZIE: Not a red cent.

FRED: It would take you far more than one night to earn five hundred bucks.

LIZZIE: Particularly if I only meet up with skinflints like you. [*Pause*] So that was why you picked me up last night? So that was it. You thought: that's the girl. I'll go home with her and start the ball rolling. So that was it! You pawed me all over but you were as cold as ice, and you were thinking: how am I going to bring her round? [*Pause*] But just a minute ... just a minute, little man ... If you came home with me to make your proposition, you didn't have to sleep with me. Hey? Why did you sleep with me, you bastard? Why did you sleep with me?

FRED: I'll be god-damned if I know. Five hundred dollars! Stop bawling! God Almighty! Five hundred dollars. Stop bawling! Stop bawling! Listen, Lizzie! Lizzie! Be reasonable! Five hundred bucks!

LIZZIE [*sobbing*]: I won't be reasonable. I don't want your five hundred bucks, I won't lie to the judge! I want to go back to New York, I want to get out of here! I want to get out of here! [*The doorbell rings. She stops abruptly. The bell rings again.*] I won't open the door.

[*Furious knocking*]

A VOICE [*off*]: Open. Police.

LIZZIE [*softly*]: The cops. I might have known. [*She shows the bracelet. She bends down and puts it back on her wrist.*] Go and hide, in the bathroom.

[*More knocking*]

THE VOICE: Police!

[FRED *doesn't move. She pushes him with all her strength.*]

THE VOICE: Are you there, Clarke? Clarke? Are you there?

FRED: I'm here! [*He pushes her away. She looks at him in amazement.*]

LIZZIE: So that's it!

[FRED *opens the door.* JOHN *and* JAMES *enter, leaving the front door open.*]

JOHN: Police. Are you Lizzie MacKay?

LIZZIE [*without hearing him, gazing at* FRED]: So that was it!

JOHN [*shaking her by the shoulder*]: Answer when you're spoken to.

LIZZIE [*recovering herself. Bitterly*]: What are you doing in my apartment? [JOHN *shows his badge.*] Anyone can carry a badge. You are this guy's pals and you're out to get me.

[JOHN *thrusts a card under her nose.*]

JOHN: Recognize that?

LIZZIE [*indicating* JAMES]: What about him?

JOHN [*to* JAMES]: Show her your card.

[JAMES *produces it.* LIZZIE *looks at it, goes to the table without a word, pulls out some papers and gives them to him.*]

JOHN [*meaning* FRED]: Did you bring him home with you last night? Don't you know prostitution is a criminal offence in this state?

LIZZIE: Are you quite sure you can come busting into people's houses without a warrant? Ain't you afraid I might make it hot for you?

JOHN: Don't worry about us. [*Pause*] I asked you if you brought this man home with you last night.

[LIZZIE *has changed since the entrance of the police officers. She has become harder and more vulgar.*]

LIZZIE: Keep your shirt on. Sure, I brought him home. Only I made love for nothing. That makes you think, don't it?

FRED: You'll find two ten-dollar bills on the table. They are mine.

LIZZIE: Prove it.

FRED [*without looking at her, to the two others*]: I got them from the bank yesterday morning, with twenty-eight others of the same serial number. You can check the numbers with the bank.

LIZZIE: I wouldn't take them. I wouldn't take his filthy money. I threw them back in his face.

JOHN: If you wouldn't take them, why are they still on the table?

LIZZIE [*after a silence*]: You've got me. [*She looks at* FRED *in a sort of stupor and says, almost gently*] So it was for this? [*To the others*] Well? What do you want me to do?

JOHN: Sit down. [*To* FRED] Did you tell her? [FRED *nods.*] I told you to sit down. [*He forces her into a chair.*] Now, the judge has agreed to release Tom if he has your written testimony. We've drawn it up for you, you've only got to sign. Tomorrow, you'll be questioned officially. Can you read? [LIZZIE *shrugs her shoulders; he holds out a paper.*] Read it and sign.

LIZZIE: It's a lie from beginning to end.

JOHN: So what?

LIZZIE: I won't sign.

FRED: Take her away. [*To* LIZZIE] It'll be eighteen months.

LIZZIE: Eighteen months, okay. And when I come out, I'll have your neck for this.

FRED: Not if I can help it. [*They look at each other.*] You should telegraph New York; I think she had a little trouble there.

LIZZIE [*admiringly*]: You're as low as a woman. I'd never have believed a man could be so low.

JOHN: Make up your mind. Sign or I take you to the courthouse.

LIZZIE: Take me. I won't lie.

FRED: You won't lie! And what else did you do all night? When you called me your darling, your love, your sweetheart, weren't you lying? When you sighed, to make me believe you liked me, weren't you lying?

LIZZIE [*defiantly*]: That would make you feel better, eh? No,

I wasn't lying. [*They look at each other.* FRED *drops his eyes.*]

FRED: Let's get this over with. Here's my pen. Sign.

LIZZIE: You can go and hang yourself.

[*Pause. The three men are embarrassed.*]

FRED: So this is what it's come to! He's the finest guy in town and his future is in the hands of this slut. [*He walks up and down, then abruptly comes back to* LIZZIE.] Look at him. [*He shows her a photograph.*] You've seen some men in your filthy life. Are there many like him? Don't worry, when he gets out of jail, in ten years' time, he'll look an old man. You can be proud of yourself, you're doing a fine job. Up to now, you've only taken the money from our pockets. This time, you've taken the pick of the bunch and you're stealing his life. Can't you say something? Are you rotten to the bone? [*He forces her to kneel.*] Kneel, you tramp!!

[SENATOR CLARKE *enters by the door they left open.*]

THE SENATOR: Let her go.

FRED: Hullo, Dad!

JOHN: Hullo, Senator!

SENATOR: Hullo, boys! [*To* LIZZIE] Please get up.

JOHN [*to* LIZZIE]: This is Senator Clarke.

SENATOR [*to* LIZZIE]: Hullo, Lizzie!

LIZZIE: Hullo!

SENATOR: Now we all know each other. That's fine. [*He looks at* LIZZIE.] Let's have a look at this young lady. She looks as though she has a kind heart.

FRED: She won't sign.

SENATOR: She is perfectly right. You enter her apartment without any authorization. [JOHN *makes a movement of protest. Emphatically*] Without the least authorization. You treat her roughly and you try to make her speak against her conscience. That's a very un-American way to behave. Did the Negro rape you, my child?

LIZZIE: No.

SENATOR: Fine. No mistake about that. Look at me. [*He looks at her.*] I'm sure she's not lying. [*Pause*] Poor Mary! [*To the others*] Well, boys, we must be getting along. There's nothing more we can do here. We must just apologize to Miss MacKay.

[FRED, JOHN, *and* JAMES *go out.*]

LIZZIE: Who's Mary?

SENATOR: Mary? My sister, the mother of our unlucky Thomas. A dear old lady. This will kill her. Good-bye, my child. [*He moves to go.*]

LIZZIE [*in a strangled voice*]: Senator! [*She rushes after him.*]

SENATOR: My child?

LIZZIE: I'm sorry.

SENATOR: Why should you be sorry, when you're telling the truth?

LIZZIE: I'm sorry the truth should be ... like that.

SENATOR: There's nothing either of us can do, and no one has the right to ask you to perjure yourself. [*Pause*] No. Don't give her another thought.

LIZZIE: Who?

SENATOR: My sister. You won't think of her, will you?

LIZZIE: Of course I will.

SENATOR: I can see through you, my child. Shall I tell you what you're thinking? [*Imitating* LIZZIE] 'If I sign, the Senator will go to her, he will say: "Lizzie MacKay is a good girl, she is giving you back your son." And she will smile through her tears, and she will say: "Lizzie MacKay? I will never forget her name." And I who have no family, whom Fate has put outside the pale of Society, I will have a little old lady, sitting in her big house, who thinks of me. There will be one American mother who has adopted me in her heart.' Poor Lizzie, forget it.

LIZZIE: Is her hair white?

SENATOR: White as snow. But her face is as young as ever. If you could only see her smile ... She will never smile again. Good-bye.

LIZZIE: Are you going?

SENATOR: Why, yes: I'm going to her. I must tell her of our conversation.

LIZZIE: She knows you're here?

SENATOR: She asked me to come.

LIZZIE: My God! She's waiting for you? And you'll tell her I refused to sign. She'll hate me for this.

SENATOR [*putting his hands on her shoulders*]: My poor child, I wouldn't like to be in your shoes.

LIZZIE: What a set-up! With things as they are, the Negro might just as well have raped me.

SENATOR [*moved*]: My poor child!

LIZZIE [*sadly*]: Yeah, you would have been so pleased, and it wouldn't have meant so much to me.

SENATOR: Thank you! [*Pause*] I wish I could help you. [*Pause*] But truth is truth.

LIZZIE [*sadly*]: Yeah.

SENATOR: And the truth is the Negro didn't rape you.

LIZZIE: That's right.

SENATOR: Yes. [*Pause*] Naturally, it's really a question of a fundamental truth.

LIZZIE [*not understanding*]: Fundamental?

SENATOR: Yes. I mean a ... primary truth.

LIZZIE: Primary? Isn't it just the truth?

SENATOR: Yes, yes, of course it's the truth. Only ... there are several degrees of truth.

LIZZIE: You think the Negro did rape me?

SENATOR: No. No. He didn't rape you. From one point of view, he didn't rape you at all. But you see, I am an old man and I've lived a long time, and made many mistakes; but these last few years, I've made fewer mistakes. And I think rather differently about this than you.

LIZZIE: How d'you mean?

SENATOR: How can I explain? Listen. Let's imagine Uncle Sam suddenly walked through that door. What do you think he would say?

LIZZIE [*frightened*]: Oh, I don't think he'd have much to say to me.

SENATOR: Are you a Communist?

LIZZIE: What an idea! Of course not!

SENATOR: Then he'd have plenty to say to you! He'd say: 'Lizzie, you've got to choose between two of my sons. One or other of them must disappear. What does one do in a case like that? You keep the better of the two. Well, let's decide which is better. Shall we?'

LIZZIE: Sure. Let's.

SENATOR: 'Lizzie, this Negro you are protecting, what use is he? He was born God knows where. I have fed him and what does he do for me in return? Nothing at all. He doesn't work, he loafs and sings all day; he buys zoot suits and fancy ties. He is my son, and I love him as a son. But I ask you; is he living a man's life? I wouldn't even notice his death.'

LIZZIE: You're a swell speaker.

SENATOR [*continuing*]: 'The other boy, this Thomas, has killed a black man, which is very bad. But I need him. He is one hundred per cent American, the son of one of our oldest families; he went to Harvard. He is an officer – and I need officers – he employs two thousand workmen in his factory – two thousand men out of a job if he dies – he is a leader of men, a solid rampart against communism, trade unionism, and the Jews. His duty is to live, and your duty is to save his life. That's all. Now choose.'

LIZZIE: How beautifully you speak.

SENATOR: Choose!

LIZZIE [*jumping*]: What? Oh yes.... [*Pause*] You've got me all mixed up. I don't know where I am any more.

SENATOR: Look at me, Lizzie. Do you trust me?

LIZZIE: Yes, Senator.

SENATOR: Do you think I would tell you to do anything wrong?

LIZZIE: No, Senator.

SENATOR: Then you must sign. Here is my pen.

LIZZIE: You think she'll be pleased with me?

SENATOR: Who?

LIZZIE: Your sister.

SENATOR: She will love you like a daughter.

LIZZIE: Perhaps she'll send me some flowers?

SENATOR: Very likely.

LIZZIE: Or a signed photograph?

SENATOR: Probably.

LIZZIE: I'd hang it on the wall. [*Pause. She walks up and down.*] What a mess! [*Coming back to the* SENATOR] What will you do to the Negro, if I sign?

SENATOR: The Negro? Bah! [*He takes her by the shoulders.*] If you sign, the whole town will adopt you. The whole town. All the mothers of the town.

LIZZIE: But ...

SENATOR: Do you think a whole town can be wrong? A whole town, with its priests and ministers, its doctors, its lawyers and painters, with its mayor and town councillors and all the charitable institutions? Do you really think so?

LIZZIE: No, no, no.

[FRED, JOHN, *and* JAMES *come in. They remain by the door.*]

SENATOR: Give me your hand. [*He forces her to sign.*] There, Lizzie. I thank you in the name of my sister and my nephew, in the name of the seventeen thousand white men of our town, in the name of Uncle Sam and the American Nation which I represent. [*He kisses her on the forehead.*] Good-bye, my child. [*To* LIZZIE] I'll see you again; we have more to say to each other. Come along, boys. [*He goes out.*]

FRED: Good-bye, Lizzie.

LIZZIE: Good-bye. [*They go out. She remains crushed, then suddenly rushes to the door.*] Senator! Senator! Come back! Tear up that paper! Senator! [*She comes back into the room, and picks up the vacuum-cleaner mechanically.*] Uncle Sam and the American Nation! [*She puts in the plug and pushes the vacuum-cleaner up and down furiously.*]

CURTAIN

*

SCENE TWO

The scene is the same. Twelve hours later. The lights are on, the windows open on the darkness. Noise outside, which grows. THE NEGRO *appears at the window, climbs over it, and jumps down into the room. He gets as far as the middle of the stage when the bell rings. He hides behind a curtain.* LIZZIE *comes out of the bathroom, goes to the front door and opens it.*

LIZZIE: Come in. [*The* SENATOR *enters.*] Well?

SENATOR: Thomas is in his mother's arms. I come to bring you their thanks.

LIZZIE: She's happy?

SENATOR: Completely happy.

LIZZIE: Sit down.

SENATOR: Thank you.

LIZZIE: Did she cry?

SENATOR: Cry? Why should she? She's a brave woman.

LIZZIE: You told me she was crying.

SENATOR: A figure of speech.

LIZZIE: She wasn't expecting it, was she? She thought I was a bad girl, and that I would stand up for the Negro.

SENATOR: She gave herself up to the mercy of God.

LIZZIE: What does she think of me?

SENATOR: She thanks you.

LIZZIE: Did she ask you what I was like?

SENATOR: No.

LIZZIE: Does she think I've behaved well?

SENATOR: She thinks you did the right thing.

LIZZIE: Yeah ...

SENATOR: She hopes you will always do the right thing.

LIZZIE: Yeah ...

SENATOR: Look at me, Lizzie. [*He takes her by the shoulders.*]

You will go on doing the right thing, won't you? You wouldn't want to disappoint her.

LIZZIE: Don't worry. I can't go back on my word; they'd put me in jug. [*Pause*] What's all that shouting?

SENATOR: Nothing.

LIZZIE: I can't bear it any more. [*She goes to the window.*] Senator?

SENATOR: My dear?

LIZZIE: You're sure we haven't made a mistake, that I have done the right thing?

SENATOR: Absolutely sure.

[*The noise outside grows louder.*]

LIZZIE: I don't know myself any more; you've mixed me all up; you think too fast for me. What's the time?

SENATOR: Eleven o'clock.

LIZZIE: Six more hours before daylight. I'll not be able to sleep tonight. [*Pause*] The nights are hotter than the days. [*Pause*] What about the Negro?

SENATOR: What Negro? Oh! Oh, yes. They're looking for him.

LIZZIE: What will they do to him, if they catch him? [*The* SENATOR *shrugs his shoulders; the tumult increases.* LIZZIE *goes to the window.*] What's all the row about? There are men down there with torches and dogs. Is it a torchlight procession? Or is it ... Tell me what it is, Senator! Tell me what they're doing!

SENATOR [*taking an envelope from his pocket*]: My sister asked me to give you this.

LIZZIE: She's written to me? [*She tears the envelope, takes out a hundred-dollar bill, looks in the envelope for a letter, doesn't find one, crumples the envelope and throws it away. Her voice changes.*] A hundred bucks. You should be delighted; your son promised me five hundred, you've saved yourself a lot of dough.

SENATOR: My dear ...

LIZZIE: You can thank your sister. Tell her I would have preferred a lipstick, or a pair of nylons, something she'd taken the trouble to choose herself. [*She throws the note away.*]

But it's the thought that counts, isn't it? [*Pause*] You fooled me beautifully.

[*Pause. They look at each other. The* SENATOR *takes a step towards her.*]

SENATOR: Lizzie, let's have a little quiet chat. You're going through a moral crisis, and you need my support.

LIZZIE: What I need is a straight Scotch, but I expect we'll understand each other, you and I. [*Pause*]

SENATOR: You know, you've got a lot of natural charm. There's something in you that all your excesses haven't spoiled. Yes. Yes. Something. [*He caresses her. She lets him, silent and scornful.*] I will come back. Don't trouble to see me out.

[*He goes out.* LIZZIE *remains rooted to the ground. But she picks up the note again, crumples it and throws it away, then sinks into a chair and bursts into tears. Outside the shouting is drawing nearer. Shots in the distance.* THE NEGRO *comes out of hiding. He stands in front of her. She lifts her head and cries out.*]

LIZZIE: Ah! [*Pause*] I was sure you'd come back. I was sure. How did you get in?

THE NEGRO: By the window.

LIZZIE: What do you want?

THE NEGRO: Hide me.

LIZZIE: I told you no.

THE NEGRO: You can hear them, mam?

LIZZIE: Yes.

THE NEGRO: That's the hunt.

LIZZIE: What hunt?

THE NEGRO: Man hunt.

LIZZIE: Ah! [*Long pause*] You're sure they didn't see you?

THE NEGRO: Sure.

LIZZIE: What will they do to you if they catch you?

THE NEGRO: Gasoline.

LIZZIE: What?

THE NEGRO: Gasoline. [*He makes an expressive gesture.*] They set fire to it.

LIZZIE: I see. Sit down. [THE NEGRO *lets himself fall into a chair.*] You had to come to me. Won't I ever be through with you? [*She goes to him, almost threateningly.*] I hate trouble, understand? [*Stamping her foot*] Hate it, hate it, hate it!

THE NEGRO: They think I done you wrong, mam.

LIZZIE: Well?

THE NEGRO: They won't look for me here.

LIZZIE: Do you know why they're hunting for you?

THE NEGRO: Because they think I done you wrong.

LIZZIE: Do you know who told them?

THE NEGRO: No.

LIZZIE: I did. [*Long pause.* THE NEGRO *looks at her.*] What do you think of that?

THE NEGRO: Why did you do that, mam? Oh, why did you do that?

LIZZIE: That's what I ask myself.

THE NEGRO: They'll have no mercy; they'll whip me over the eyes, they'll pour cans of gasoline over me. Oh, why did you do that? I didn't do nothing to you.

LIZZIE: Oh yes, you did. You've no idea what you've done to me! [*Pause*] Don't you want to break my neck?

THE NEGRO: They often make folk say what they don't think.

LIZZIE: Yes. Often. And when they can't, they mix them up with their pretty stories. [*Pause*] Well? Don't you want to break my neck? You're a good soul. [*Pause*] I'll hide you until tomorrow night. [*He makes a movement.*] Don't touch me; I don't like black men. [*Shouts and shots nearer*] They're getting nearer. [*She switches off the light, goes to the window, parts the curtains, and looks down into the street.*] We're caught.

THE NEGRO: What are they doing?

LIZZIE: They've got sentinels at each end of the street and they're searching all the houses. You just had to come here, didn't you? Somebody must have seen you in the street. [*She looks again.*] Now. It's our turn. They're coming upstairs.

THE NEGRO: How many of them?

LIZZIE: Five or six. The others are waiting below. [*She goes back to him.*] Don't shake like that! Christ, don't shake like that. [*Pause. She throws her bracelet on the ground and stamps on it.*] You did right to come here. [*He gets up and moves as if to go.*] Sit still. If you go out, we're done for.

THE NEGRO: The roof.

LIZZIE: With this moon? You can try if you want to be drilled full of holes. [*Pause*] Wait. They've got two floors to search before they get here. [*Long pause. She paces up and down.* THE NEGRO *stays huddled in his chair.*] Have you got a gun?

THE NEGRO: Oh, no!

LIZZIE: Fine. [*She goes to a suitcase and gets out a revolver.*]

THE NEGRO: What are you going to do, mam?

LIZZIE: I'm going to open the door and ask them to come in. For twenty-five years they've fooled me. White-haired mothers! Heroes! Uncle Sam and the American Nation! Now I understand. They won't catch me out again! I'll open the door, and I'll say: 'He's here. He's here, but he has done nothing. I was forced to sign a false statement. I swear by Almighty God that he didn't do anything.'

THE NEGRO: They won't believe you.

LIZZIE: Maybe. Maybe they won't believe me: then you'll aim the gun and if they don't go away, you'll fire.

THE NEGRO: Others will come.

LIZZIE: You must shoot them too. And if you see the Senator's son, try not to miss him, because he worked the whole thing. We're done for, I tell you. We're done for either way, I tell you. If they find you here, I wouldn't give a button for my skin. So we might as well die in good company. [*She holds out the revolver.*] Take it! Take it, I tell you!

THE NEGRO: I can't, mam.

LIZZIE: What?

THE NEGRO: I can't shoot a white man.

LIZZIE: They won't be so soft.

THE NEGRO: They are white folk, mam.

LIZZIE: So what? Just because they're white, have they the right to hound you like a dog?

THE NEGRO: They are white folk.

LIZZIE: Hide in the bathroom.

[THE NEGRO *obeys.* LIZZIE *waits. The bell rings. She crosses herself, picks up the bracelet, and opens the door. Several* MEN *are there with guns.*]

FIRST MAN: We're looking for the nigger.

LIZZIE: What nigger?

FIRST MAN: The one who raped a white woman in the train and slashed the Senator's nephew with a razor.

LIZZIE: You shouldn't come looking for him here. [*Pause*] Don't you know me?

SECOND MAN: Yes. I saw you getting out of the train the day before yesterday.

LIZZIE: I'm the girl he raped, see?

[*Sensation. They look at her with astonishment, desire, and a sort of horror. They draw back slightly. Pause. They laugh.*]

A MAN: Would you like to see him hang, sister?

LIZZIE: Come and fetch me when you've got him.

A MAN: Won't be long now, sugar.

ANOTHER MAN: We know he's hiding in the street.

LIZZIE: Good luck. [*They go out. She closes the door. Then she puts the revolver down on the bed.*] You can come out, now. [THE NEGRO *comes out, kneels down, and kisses the hem of her dress.*] I told you not to touch me. [*She looks at him.*] You must be a funny sort of bastard to have the whole town after you.

THE NEGRO: I ain't done nothin', mam, you know that.

LIZZIE: They say a Negro has always done something.

THE NEGRO: I ain't done nothin'.

LIZZIE [*she passes her hand over her forehead*]: I don't know where I am. [*Pause*] All the same, a whole town, they can't all be wrong. ... [*Pause*] Damn! I don't understand any more.

THE NEGRO: It's like that, mam. It's always like that with white folk.

LIZZIE: Do you feel guilty too?

THE NEGRO: Yes, mam.

LIZZIE: And you've done nothing?

THE NEGRO: No, mam.

LIZZIE: But why is one always on their side?

THE NEGRO: They're white folk.

LIZZIE: I'm white too. [*Pause. Footsteps outside*] It's all right. They're going away again. [*She goes to him instinctively. He is trembling, but he puts his arm round her shoulders. The steps die away. Silence. She frees herself abruptly.*] Gee! We must have looked lonely. Like a couple of orphans. [*The bell rings. They listen in silence. The bell rings again.*] Go into the bathroom. [*Someone begins to hammer on the door.* THE NEGRO *hides.* LIZZIE *opens the door. It is* FRED.] Are you crazy? Why are you banging on my door like that? No, you can't come in. [*He pushes her to one side, switches on the lights, shuts the door, and takes her by the shoulders. Long silence*] Well?

FRED: They caught a nigger. It wasn't the right one. They lynched him all the same.

LIZZIE: So?

FRED: I was with them.

[LIZZIE *whistles.*]

LIZZIE: I see. [*Pause*] They say it's quite something, to see a Negro lynched.

FRED: I want you.

LIZZIE: What?

FRED: You're the devil! You've bewitched me. I was in the midst of them, I had my revolver in my hand, and the nigger was out on a branch. I looked at him, and thought, I want her. It isn't natural.

LIZZIE: Let me go. Let me go, I say.

FRED: What does it mean? What have you done to me, you witch? I looked at the nigger and I saw you. I saw you standing above the flames. I fired.

LIZZIE: You bastard! Let me go! Let me go! Murderer.

FRED: What have you done to me? You cling as closely as my teeth to my gums. [*Forces her on to the bed*] I see you everywhere, I see your body, your wicked body, I feel your warmth between my hands, I have your scent in my nostrils. I've run all the way here, I didn't know if it was to kill you or take you by force. Now I know. [*He lets her go abruptly and then comes back to her.*] Was it true what you said, this morning?

LIZZIE: What?

FRED: That you liked me?

LIZZIE: Leave me alone.

FRED: Swear that it's true. Swear! [*He twists her wrist. Cry. There is a noise in the bathroom.*] What is it? [*He listens.*] There's someone here.

LIZZIE: You're crazy. There's no one.

FRED: Yes, there is. In the bathroom. [*He goes towards it.*]

LIZZIE: You can't go in there.

FRED: Of course there's someone.

LIZZIE: It's a client. A guy with dough.

FRED: A client? You'll have no more clients. Never. You're mine. [*Pause*] I'd like to see him. [*He shouts*] Come out of there!

LIZZIE [*shouting*]: Don't come out. It's a trap.

FRED: Come out of there. [*He pushes her violently away, goes to the door and opens it.* THE NEGRO *comes out.*] Is this your client?

LIZZIE: Don't fire. You know he's innocent.

[FRED *pulls out his gun. Suddenly* THE NEGRO *springs forward, pushes him aside and runs away.* FRED *goes after him.* LIZZIE *goes to the door through which they have disappeared and begins to shout.*]

LIZZIE: He's innocent! Innocent! [*Two shots. She turns, her face set and hard. She goes to the table, takes up the revolver.* FRED *comes back. She turns towards him, back to the audience, holding her gun behind her back. He throws his on the table.*] Did you get him? [FRED *does not answer.*] Fine. Well, now it's your turn. [*She aims the revolver at him.*]

FRED: Lizzie! Think of my mother.

LIZZIE: To hell with your mother! I've been had that way already.

FRED [*walking slowly towards her*]: The first Clarke cleared a forest with his own hands: he shot sixteen Indians before being killed himself in an ambush. His son built nearly the whole of this town; he was Washington's friend and died at Yorktown, fighting for the independence of the United States. My great-grandfather was a Vigilante in San Francisco; he saved twenty-two lives during the great fire. My grandfather came to live here; he dug a canal to the Mississippi and was Governor of the state. My father is a senator; I shall be a senator after him; I am his only male heir and the last of my name. We have made this country and its story is our story. There have been Clarkes in Alaska, in the Philippines, in New Mexico. Dare you shoot the whole of America?

LIZZIE: If you come closer, I fire!

FRED: Fire! Fire! You see, you cannot. A girl like you cannot kill a man like me. Who are you? What can you do? Do you even know your grandfather's name? I have the right to live: there are so many things to do, waiting for me to do them. Give me that gun.

[*She gives it to him. He puts it in his pocket.*]

FRED: The nigger ran too fast; I missed him. [*Pause. He puts his arm round her shoulders.*] I'll buy you a house up on the hill, on the other side of the river, a fine house with a garden. You can walk in the garden, but I forbid you to go out; I'm very jealous. I'll come and see you three times a week, in the evening; Tuesdays, Thursdays and week-ends. You'll have coloured servants and more money than you ever dreamed of, but you must do everything I want. And I want plenty! [*She lets herself relax a little in his arms.*] Did you really like me? Tell me. Did you?

LIZZIE [*drowsily*]: Yes, I did.

FRED [*tapping her cheek*]: Then everything's fine. [*Pause*] You can call me Fred.

CURTAIN

LUCIFER AND THE LORD

CHARACTERS

GOETZ
HEINRICH
NASTI
TETZEL
KARL
HEINZ
THE ARCHBISHOP
SCHMIDT
GERLACH
THE BANKER
A PROPHET
THE BISHOP OF WORMS
FRANZ
SCHULHEIM
NOSSAK
REITSCHEL
} Barons
HILDA
CATHERINE
A WOMAN
A WITCH

Officers, Soldiers, Citizens, Peasants and Servants

Act 1

SCENE ONE

Left, between heaven and earth, a hall in the Archbishop's palace. Right, the Bishop's palace and the ramparts of the town of Worms. For the moment, only the Archbishop's palace is visible, the rest being lost in shadows.

THE ARCHBISHOP [*at his window*]: Will he come? Oh Lord; on my coinage, the thumbs of my subjects have worn away image and inscription: now Thy terrible thumb is wearing away my flesh and blood. I am no more than the shadow of an archbishop. Should the close of this day bring the news of my defeat, I shall become transparent, so great is Thy usance. And then, oh Lord, what good shall I be as Thy servant? [*A servant enters.*] Is it Linehart?

THE SERVANT: No, your Eminence. The banker Foucre. He is asking ...

THE ARCHBISHOP: Later. [*Pause*] What is Linehart doing? He should be here with fresh news. [*Pause*] Do they talk of the battle in the kitchens?

THE SERVANT: They talk of nothing else, my lord.

THE ARCHBISHOP: What are they saying?

THE SERVANT: That our prospects are excellent. Conrad is caught between the mountains and the river, and ...

THE ARCHBISHOP: I know, I know. But if a man fights a battle, he may also lose a battle.

THE SERVANT: Your Eminence ...

THE ARCHBISHOP: Leave me. [*The* SERVANT *goes.*] My Lord, why hast Thou permitted this? The enemy invades my lands, and my faithful town of Worms revolts against me while I am engaging Conrad. They dared strike me in the back. I did not know, Lord, that such great things were reserved for Thy servant. Must I wander from door to door, a blind beggar, led by a little child? I am ready to obey, if such be Thy holy will. But remember, O Lord, I pray You, that I am no longer young and I never had a real vocation as a martyr.

[*In the distance cries of* '*Victory! Victory!*' *The* ARCHBISHOP *listens, and lays his hand on his heart.*]

THE SERVANT [*entering*]: Victory! Victory! We have won a great victory, my lord. Colonel Linehart has arrived.

LINEHART [*entering*]: Victory, your Eminence. Victory. Complete and classic. A model battle. A historical achievement. The enemy loses six thousand killed or drowned, the rest are in flight.

THE ARCHBISHOP: Thanks be to God. And Conrad?

LINEHART: Among the dead.

THE ARCHBISHOP: Thanks be to God. [*Pause*] If he is dead, then I forgive him. [*To* LINEHART] I give you my blessing. Go out and spread the news.

LINEHART [*full of enthusiasm*]: A little after sunrise, we were aware of a cloud of dust ...

THE ARCHBISHOP [*interrupting*]: No, no! No details! Never bother me with details. A victory described in detail is indistinguishable from a defeat. At least, this time it really is a victory?

LINEHART: A pearl of a victory; real style and elegance.

THE ARCHBISHOP: Leave me now. I must pray. [LINEHART *goes.* THE ARCHBISHOP *begins to caper round the room.*] I've won! I've won! [*His hand on his heart*] Ooh! [*He falls on his knees on his prie-dieu.*] Let us pray.

[*Part of the stage lights up on the right. Ramparts and a sentinel's post.* HEINZ *and* SCHMIDT *are sitting on the crenellations.*]

HEINZ: I don't believe it. ... I don't believe it. God would never allow it.

SCHMIDT: Wait. They'll begin again. See! One – two – three ... Three ... and one – two – three – four – five ...

NASTI [*appearing on the ramparts*]: What's the matter?

SCHMIDT: Nasti! We've had bad news.

NASTI: For God's elect the news is never bad.

HEINZ: For more than an hour, we've been watching the signal-fires. Once every minute they repeat the message, and it's always the same one. See! One – two – three – three and five. [*He points to the mountain.*] The Archbishop has won a battle.

NASTI: I know.

SCHMIDT: The situation is desperate; we are trapped here in Worms without allies and without supplies. You told us Goetz would finally lose patience and raise the siege, that Conrad would destroy the Archbishop. Well, Conrad is dead, the Archbishop's armies can join with Goetz's troops before our walls. There is nothing we can do but die.

GERLACH [*entering, running*]: Conrad is beaten. The Burgomaster and elders of the city are meeting at the Town Hall.

SCHMIDT: God's blood! They must be considering how to surrender the city.

NASTI: Is your faith strong, my brothers?

ALL: Yes, Nasti, yes!

NASTI: Then fear nothing. Conrad's defeat is a sign.

SCHMIDT: A sign?

NASTI: A sign that God has sent me. Gerlach, go to the Town Hall, and try to find out what the Council has decided.

[*The ramparts disappear into the night.*]

THE ARCHBISHOP [*rising*]: Hola! [*The* SERVANT *appears.*] Bring in the banker. [*The* BANKER *enters.*] Be seated, master banker. You are covered with dust. What brings you here?

THE BANKER: I have travelled thirty-six hours without pause to prevent you committing a folly.

THE ARCHBISHOP: A folly?

THE BANKER: You are about to kill a goose that every year lays you a golden egg.

THE ARCHBISHOP: What are you talking about?

THE BANKER: Your city of Worms. I am told you are besieging it. If your troops sack the city, you will ruin yourself, and me besides. Is playing soldiers a fit game at your time of life?

THE ARCHBISHOP: It was not I who provoked Conrad.

THE BANKER: Perhaps not. But who can tell me that you didn't provoke him to provoke you?

THE ARCHBISHOP: He was my vassal and he owed me obedience. But the Devil whispered to him to incite the knights to revolt and place himself at their head.

THE BANKER: Why didn't you accede to his demands before he lost patience?

THE ARCHBISHOP: He was demanding everything.

THE BANKER: Very well, let us overlook Conrad. He was obviously the aggressor, since he has now been defeated. But your noble town of Worms ...

THE ARCHBISHOP: Worms, my jewel, Worms, my delight, Worms, the ungrateful, revolted against me the very day Conrad crossed the frontier.

THE BANKER: It was a heavy sin. But three-quarters of your revenues come from Worms. Who will pay your taxes, who will reimburse my loans if you massacre your citizens like a venerable Tiberius?

THE ARCHBISHOP: They have molested the priests and forced them to take refuge in their monasteries. They have insulted my bishop and forbidden him to leave his palace.

THE BANKER: Childish nonsense! They would never have taken up arms if you had not forced them to it. Violence is only proper for those who have nothing to lose.

THE ARCHBISHOP: What do you want of me?

THE BANKER: First, your forgiveness. Let them pay you a good, fat fine, and forget the whole business.

THE ARCHBISHOP: Alas!

THE BANKER: What do you mean, alas?

THE ARCHBISHOP: I love my city, banker. Even without a fine, I forgive it with all my heart.

THE BANKER: Well, then?

THE ARCHBISHOP: It is no longer I who is besieging Worms.

THE BANKER: Then who is?

THE ARCHBISHOP: Goetz.

THE BANKER: Which Goetz? Conrad's brother?

THE ARCHBISHOP: Yes. The finest captain in all Germany.

THE BANKER: What is he doing outside the walls of your city? I thought he was your ally?

THE ARCHBISHOP: To tell you the truth, I don't really know

what he is. First, he was Conrad's ally and my foe, then he was Conrad's foe and my ally. Now ... He has a changing humour, which is the least one can say of him.

THE BANKER: Why choose yourself such doubtful allies?

THE ARCHBISHOP: What choice did I have? He and Conrad invaded my territories. Luckily, I discovered there was a rift between them, and I promised Goetz in secret that he should have his brother's lands if he would join with me. If I had not won him away from Conrad, I should have lost this war a long time ago.

THE BANKER: So he came over to you with all his forces. And then?

THE ARCHBISHOP: I gave him command of the frontier posts. He must have grown tired of waiting, or perhaps he does not like a garrison life. One morning he appeared beneath the walls of Worms with all his army, and began the siege without a word of reference to me.

THE BANKER: Order him ... [*The* ARCHBISHOP *smiles sadly and shrugs his shoulders.*] He doesn't obey you?

THE ARCHBISHOP: What general in the field obeys his political leader?

THE BANKER: So we are entirely at his mercy?

THE ARCHBISHOP: Yes. Entirely.

[*The ramparts again become visible.*]

GERLACH [*entering*]: The Council has decided to send a deputation to Goetz.

HEINZ: So that's it. [*Pause*] The swine.

GERLACH: Our only hope will be that Goetz demands impossible conditions. If he is the man they say he is, he won't even accept complete surrender.

THE BANKER: Perhaps he will spare the city's treasures.

THE ARCHBISHOP: Not even one life, I'm afraid.

SCHMIDT [*to* GERLACH]: But why? Why?

THE ARCHBISHOP: He is a bastard – and of the worst kind. On his mother's side. He takes no pleasure in anything but evil.

GERLACH: He's a swine too, a bastard; he enjoys evil. If he wants to sack Worms, our citizens will have to fight with their backs to the wall.

SCHMIDT: If he wants to raze the city, he wouldn't be fool enough to say so. He'll demand free entry, and promise not to touch a feather.

THE BANKER [*indignantly*]: Worms owes me thirty thousand ducats. We must put an end to all this nonsense. Set your forces in motion against Goetz.

THE ARCHBISHOP [*overcome*]: I'm afraid he may beat them for me.

[*The Archbishop's palace disappears.*]

HEINZ [*to* NASTI]: Then there is really no hope for us?

NASTI: God is with us, my brothers; we cannot lose. Tonight I will leave Worms and try to cross the camp and reach Waldorf. In a week, I can have ten thousand peasants under arms.

SCHMIDT: But how can we hold out for a week? They are capable of opening the gates to him this very night.

NASTI: They mustn't be allowed to open them.

HEINZ: Do you want to seize command?

NASTI: No. The situation is too uncertain.

HEINZ: Well, then?

NASTI: We must compromise the citizens in such a way that they'll fight for their very lives.

ALL: How?

NASTI: By a murder.

[*Below the ramparts, the scene lights up. A woman is sitting against the stairway which leads up to the sentinel's post. She is thirty-five and dressed in rags. She gazes ahead of her in stony silence. A priest passes, reading his breviary.*]

NASTI: Who is that priest? Why isn't he shut up with the others?

HEINZ: Don't you know him?

NASTI: Ah, yes. It is Heinrich. How changed he is. Nevertheless, he should have been imprisoned.

HEINZ: The poor love him because he lives as they do. We were afraid to anger the poor people.

NASTI: He is the most dangerous of all.

THE WOMAN [*seeing the priest*]: Father! Father! [*The priest tries to escape; she cries after him*] Where are you going so fast?

HEINRICH [*stopping*]: I have nothing left! Nothing! Nothing. I have given everything away.

THE WOMAN: That's no reason to run away when someone calls you.

HEINRICH [*coming back towards her, very tired*]: You are hungry?

THE WOMAN: No.

HEINRICH: Then what do you want?

THE WOMAN: I want you to explain.

HEINRICH [*quickly*]: I refuse to explain anything.

THE WOMAN: You don't even know what I want to ask you.

HEINRICH: Very well. Quickly. What do you want me to explain?

THE WOMAN: Why the child died.

HEINRICH: What child?

THE WOMAN [*laughing a little*]: My child. Don't you remember? You buried him yesterday. He was three years old, and he had died of hunger.

HEINRICH: I am tired, my sister, and I didn't recognize you. To me, all you women seem alike, with terrible eyes ...

THE WOMAN: Why did he die?

HEINRICH: I cannot tell you.

THE WOMAN: And yet you are a priest.

HEINRICH: Yes.

THE WOMAN: Then who can tell me, if you cannot? [*Pause*] If I were to let myself die now would it be a sin?

HEINRICH [*forcefully*]: Yes. A great sin.

THE WOMAN: That's what I thought. And yet, I should so much like to die. You see, you really must explain.

[*Pause.* HEINRICH *rubs his forehead, and makes a great effort.*]

HEINRICH: Nothing on earth occurs without the will of God. And God is goodness itself, therefore everything happens for the best.

THE WOMAN: I don't understand.

HEINRICH: God knows more than you can understand. What seems misfortune is a blessing in His eyes because He weighs up all the consequences.

THE WOMAN: Do you understand?

HEINRICH: No! No! I don't understand! I understand nothing!

I neither can nor want to understand. We must believe – believe – believe!

THE WOMAN [*with a little laugh*]: You say we must believe and you don't look as though you yourself believe what you are saying.

HEINRICH: My sister, I have said the same words so often these last three months, I no longer know if I say them out of conviction or from habit. But make no mistake. I believe. I believe with all my strength and with all my heart. My God, I call you to witness that not for one moment has my heart been compromised by doubt. [*Pause*] Woman, your child is in heaven, and you will be reunited with him there. [*He kneels.*]

THE WOMAN: Yes, father, of course. But heaven is different. And I'm so tired, I shall never rejoice again. Not even in heaven.

HEINRICH: My sister, forgive me.

THE WOMAN: Why should I forgive you, good father? You have done me no harm.

HEINRICH: Forgive me. Forgive in me all the other priests – all those who are rich, as well as all those who are poor.

THE WOMAN [*amused*]: I forgive you with all my heart. Does that satisfy you?

HEINRICH: Yes. Now, my sister, let us pray together. Pray to God to give us back our hope.

[*During the last lines,* NASTI *slowly comes down from the ramparts.*]

THE WOMAN [*seeing* NASTI *and interrupting herself, joyfully*]: Nasti! Nasti the Baker!

NASTI: What do you want?

THE WOMAN: Nasti, my child is dead. You must be able to say why, you who know everything.

NASTI: Yes – I know.

HEINRICH: Nasti – I implore you, say nothing. Woe to those through whom the error arises.

NASTI: He died because the rich burghers of our city revolted against the Archbishop, their very rich overlord. When the rich fight the rich, it is the poor who have to die.

THE WOMAN: Was it God's will that they should begin this war?

NASTI: God had commanded them not to begin it.

THE WOMAN: This man says nothing happens except by the will of God.

NASTI: Nothing, except evil, which is born of the wickedness of man.

HEINRICH: Nasti, you are lying. You confuse the false and the true in order to betray the souls of men.

NASTI: Dare you assert that God permits this mourning and this useless suffering? I say that God is innocent of our sins.

[HEINRICH *is silent.*]

THE WOMAN: Then it was not the will of God that my child should die?

NASTI: If He desired his death, why should God have created him?

THE WOMAN [*consoled*]: I think that is much better. [*To* HEINRICH] You see, when he says that, I understand. You mean, God is sad too, when He sees how I am suffering?

NASTI: Sad unto death.

THE WOMAN: And He can do nothing for me?

NASTI: Of course He can. He can give you back your son.

THE WOMAN [*disappointed*]: Yes, I know. In heaven!

NASTI: No, not in heaven. Here on earth.

THE WOMAN [*surprised*]: On earth?

NASTI: You must first pass through the eye of a needle, and endure for seven years. Then the kingdom of God will be established on earth; our dead will arise, all men will love one another, and those who hunger will be filled.

THE WOMAN: Why must we wait seven years?

NASTI: Because we shall need seven years of endeavour to drive out the wicked.

THE WOMAN: The task is very hard.

NASTI: That is why God needs your help.

THE WOMAN: God the All-Powerful needs my help?

NASTI: Yes, my sister. For seven more years, the Evil One will reign on earth; but if each one of us fights with all his strength, we shall redeem all men, and God will be redeemed too. Do you believe me?

THE WOMAN [*rising*]: Yes, Nasti; I believe you.

NASTI: Your child is not in heaven, woman. He is within you, and you will carry him for seven long years. Then he will walk at your side, holding your hand in his hand, and you will have brought him into the world a second time.

THE WOMAN: I believe you, Nasti. I believe you. [*She goes out.*]

HEINRICH: You have damned her for ever.

NASTI: If you believe that, why didn't you stop me?

HEINRICH: Ah! Because she seemed a little less unhappy. [NASTI *shrugs his shoulders.*] Oh Lord, I lacked courage to silence this blasphemer; I have sinned. But I believe, oh Lord, I believe in Thy omnipotence; I believe in Thy Holy Church, my mother, the sacred body of Jesus of which I am a member; I believe that nothing occurs except by Thy laws, even the death of a little child, and that all is well done. I believe because it is absurd! Absurd! Absurd!

[*The whole stage lights up. Citizens with their wives are grouped around the Bishop's palace, waiting for him to come out.*]

VOICES:

- Is there any news?
- No news.
- What are we doing here?
- Waiting.
- What are we waiting for?
- Nothing ...
- Did you see? ...
- Over there ...
- The ugly brutes.
- When the water is stirred, the mud rises ...
- A man isn't at home in the streets any more ...
- We must end this war – we must end it soon. If not, disasters will occur.
- I want to see the Bishop – I want to see the Bishop ...
- He won't appear ... He is angry ...
- Who? ... Who? ...
- The Bishop.

– Since he has been imprisoned here, sometimes he comes to the window. He draws aside the curtain and watches us.
– He doesn't look like a good man.
– What do you expect him to say?
– He may have had news.

[*Murmurs from the crowd, which grow into isolated shouts:*]

– Bishop! Bishop! Come out! ... Show yourself! ...
– Advise us.
– What is to happen?
– It's the end of the world!

[*A man springs from out of the crowd, rushes to the façade of the Bishop's palace and sets his back against it.* HEINRICH *draws aside from him, and rejoins the crowd.*]

THE PROPHET: The world is betrayed! Betrayed!
We must chastise the flesh!
Arise, arise, arise; the Lord is there.

[*Cries, the beginning of a panic.*]

A CITIZEN: Quiet – quiet! It is nothing but a prophet.

THE CROWD: Another prophet! We've had enough prophets! We don't want to listen. They are springing up everywhere. What's the good of imprisoning the priests?

THE PROPHET: Earth has its odours ...
The sun complained to the Lord!
Oh, Lord, let me put out my light,
I have suffered this putrefaction enough.
The more I warm it with my rays, the higher its stink rises.
The stink of the earth sullies my golden rays.
Woe, woe, cries the sun. My fair circlet of sunlight has been dragged in the mire.

A CITIZEN: Shut your trap!

[*The prophet falls to the ground. The window of the palace is flung open. The* BISHOP *appears on the balcony in full regalia.*]

THE CROWD: The Bishop!

THE BISHOP: Where are the armies of Conrad? Where are his knights with their armour? Where is the legion of angels to put the enemy to flight? You are friendless, alone, without hope and damned for ever. Answer me, citizens of Worms, answer; if you believe you are serving God by imprisoning

His ministers, why has the Lord abandoned you? [*Groans from the crowd*] Answer me!

HEINRICH: Do not destroy their courage.

THE BISHOP: Who speaks?

HEINRICH: It is I, Heinrich, the parish priest of Saint Gilhau.

THE BISHOP: Swallow your tongue, priest apostate. Dare you look on the face of your bishop?

HEINRICH: If they have sinned against you, my lord, forgive them their trespasses, as I forgive you these insults.

THE BISHOP: Judas! Judas Iscariot! Hang thyself!

HEINRICH: I am no Judas.

THE BISHOP: Then what is your business among them? Why do you plead for them! Why are you not imprisoned with your fellows?

HEINRICH: They allowed me to go free because they know that I love them. If I have not joined the other priests of my own free will, it was to ensure that masses would be said and the holy sacraments given in this lost city. Without me, the Church would be absent, Worms delivered defenceless to the powers of heresy, and its children would die like beasts of the field. ... My lord, do not destroy their courage.

THE BISHOP: Who fed you? Who brought you up? Who taught you to read? Who gave you your knowledge? Who consecrated you priest?

HEINRICH: The Church, my holy Mother.

THE BISHOP: You owe the Church everything. You belong to the Church.

HEINRICH: I belong to the Church, but I am also their brother.

THE BISHOP [*violently*]: The Church must be served first.

HEINRICH: Yes. The Church must be served first, but ...

THE BISHOP: I shall speak to these people. If they persist in their errors and continue in their rebellion, I command you to rejoin the men of the Church, your true brothers, and to take your place with them at the monastery, or in the Seminary. Will you obey your Bishop?

A VOICE FROM THE PEOPLE: You mustn't leave us, Heinrich. You are the priest of the poor – you belong to us.

HEINRICH [*overcome, but in a firm voice*]: The Church must be served first. My lord Bishop, I will obey.

THE BISHOP: People of Worms, behold your fair and flourishing city; look at it closely. Look at it for the last time. It will become an infected centre of famine and plague; and as a last horror, the rich and the poor will massacre each other. When the soldiers of Goetz enter the city, they will find nothing but rotting corpses and skeletons. [*Pause*] I alone can save you, but you must know how to soften my heart.

VOICES: Save us – my lord Bishop – save us!

THE BISHOP: On your knees, proud burghers, and ask pardon of God! [*The burghers kneel down one after the other. The people remain standing.*] Heinrich! Will you kneel? [HEINRICH *kneels.*] Repeat after me: Lord God of heaven, forgive us our trespasses and soften the wrath of our holy Bishop.

THE CROWD: Lord God of Heaven, forgive us our trespasses, and soften the wrath of our holy Bishop.

THE BISHOP: Amen. You may rise. [*Pause*] First, you will free the priests and the nuns, then you will open the gates of the city. You will kneel in the square outside the cathedral and wait there in humble repentance. Meanwhile, we shall go in procession to Goetz to beg him to spare your lives.

A CITIZEN: What if he refuses to hear you?

THE BISHOP: Above the power of Goetz is the power of the Archbishop. He is our holy father, and his justice will be paternal.

[*For some moments,* NASTI *has been standing on the ramparts. He listens, in silence, then, on the last words, he comes down two steps of the stairs.*]

NASTI: Goetz does not serve the Archbishop. Goetz serves the Devil. He swore an oath to Conrad his brother, and in spite of that, he betrayed him. If he promises to spare your lives today, will you be fools enough to believe him?

THE BISHOP: You, whoever you are, I command you ...

NASTI: Who are you to give me orders? And you, do you need to listen? You need no orders from anyone, except from the leaders you have chosen yourselves.

THE BISHOP: And who chose you, ragamuffin?

NASTI: The people. [*To the others*] The soldiers are on our side. I have stationed my men at the gates. If anyone tries to open them – death.

THE BISHOP: Courage, unhappy man. You are driving them to perdition. They had only one chance of safety, and you have taken that chance away from them.

NASTI: If there were no hope, I should be the first to counsel you to surrender. But who dare say God has abandoned us? Do they ask you to doubt the angels? My brothers, I tell you, the angels are there! Do not lift up your eyes – the heavens are empty. The angels are at work on this earth; they have attacked the enemy camp.

A CITIZEN: What angels?

NASTI: The angel of cholera, and the angel of pestilence – the angel of famine and the angel of discord. Hold fast – only hold fast, my brothers. The city is impregnable and God is on our side. The siege will be raised.

THE BISHOP: Citizens of Worms, those who listen to this heresy are damned to perdition. I swear it by my place in Paradise.

NASTI: Your place in Paradise? God has divided it among the dogs.

THE BISHOP: He is holding yours ready for you, warm and waiting, till the moment you come and fetch it. He must rejoice at this moment as He hears you insulting His priest.

NASTI: Who ordained you priest?

THE BISHOP: The Holy Church.

NASTI: Your Holy Church is a whore; she sells her favours to the rich. Must I make confession to you? Accept remission of my sins at your hands? Your soul is stricken with leprosy, God grinds His teeth when He beholds it. My brothers, we have no further need of priests; any man can perform the rite of baptism; any man on earth can grant absolution; all men possess the divine right to preach. I tell you truly; all men on earth are prophets, or God does not exist.

THE BISHOP: Woe! Woe! Anathema! [*He hurls his cross at his face.*]

NASTI [*pointing to the door of the palace*]: This door is worm-eaten; a single blow would split it in pieces. [*Silence*] How patient you are, my brothers. [*Pause. To the people*] They are men of rags; the Bishop, the Council, the rich burghers. They would surrender the city because they are afraid of the people. And who will pay for all if they surrender? You! Always you! Come, arise, my brothers. We must kill to earn our place in heaven.

[*The men of the people murmur.*]

A BURGHER [*to his wife*]: Come! Let us go.

ANOTHER [*to his son*]: Quick! We must bar the shutters and barricade the shop.

THE BISHOP: My God, I call You to witness that I have done what I could to save my people. I shall die without regrets in Thy glory, for I know now that Thy anger will be drawn down on Worms and grind the city to powder.

NASTI: This dotard will devour you alive. Why is his voice so strong? Because he eats his fill every day. Go and search his granaries; you'll find enough wheat to feed a regiment for six months.

THE BISHOP [*in a powerful voice*]: You lie. My storehouse is empty, and you know it.

NASTI: Why not see, my brothers? Why not see? Will you believe his mere word?

[*The citizens withdraw hastily. The men of the people remain with* NASTI.]

HEINRICH [*going to* NASTI]: Nasti!

NASTI: What do you want?

HEINRICH: You know that his storehouses are empty. You know he hardly touches food, that he gives all he receives to the poor.

NASTI: Are you for us or against us?

HEINRICH: I am for you when you suffer, but against you when you wish to shed the blood of the Church.

NASTI: You are for us when we are massacred, against us when we fight for our lives.

HEINRICH: I belong to the Church, Nasti.

NASTI: Drive in the door!

[*A group of men attack the door. The* BISHOP *prays in silence, erect, motionless.*]

HEINRICH [*throwing himself in front of the door*]: You will have to kill me …

A MAN OF THE PEOPLE: Kill you? Why?

[*They strike him, and throw him to the ground.*]

HEINRICH: You struck me! I loved you more than my own soul, and you struck me. Not the Bishop, Nasti, not the Bishop! Kill me if you will, but spare the Bishop.

NASTI: Why not? He has starved the people.

HEINRICH: You know that is false! You know it! You know it! If you desire to free your brothers from oppression and falsehood, why begin by telling them lies?

NASTI: I never lie.

HEINRICH: You are lying. There is no corn in his storehouse.

NASTI: What does it matter? There are precious stones and gold in his churches. I say he is responsible for the deaths of all those who have died of hunger at the feet of his Christs in marble and his ivory Virgins.

HEINRICH: It isn't the same. You may not be telling a lie, but you are not telling the truth, either.

NASTI: You speak the truth of your people – I speak the truth of our own. And if God loves the poor, it is our truth which He will make His own on the day of Judgement.

HEINRICH: Then let Him judge the Bishop. But do not shed the blood of the Church.

NASTI: I only recognize one church; the community of men.

HEINRICH: All men, then, all Christians joined together by love. But you will inaugurate your society by murder.

NASTI: It is too early to love all men. We shall buy that right by shedding blood.

HEINRICH: God has forbidden violence; it is an abomination.

NASTI: And Hell? Do the damned not suffer violence?

HEINRICH: God has said: He who takes the sword …

NASTI: By the sword shall he perish … Very well – let us perish by the sword. We shall perish, but our sons will see His kingdom established on earth. Let me go. You are the same as all the others.

HEINRICH: Nasti! Nasti! Why cannot you love me? What have I done to you?

NASTI: You are a priest, and a priest remains a priest whatever he may do.

HEINRICH: I am one of yourselves. A poor man, and the son of a poor father.

NASTI: That proves you a traitor – that is all.

HEINRICH [*crying out*]: They have broken the door down! [*The door has indeed given way, and men are pouring into the palace.* HEINRICH *falls on his knees.*] Dear God, if Thou lovest mankind, if Thy face is not yet set against them, stretch forth Thy power, prevent this murder.

THE BISHOP: I have no need of your prayers, Heinrich! All you who know not what you do, receive my forgiveness. But you, priest apostate, shall inherit my curse.

HEINRICH: Ah! [*He falls to the ground.*]

THE BISHOP: Alleluia! Alleluia! Alleluia! [*He is struck down, and falls in a heap on the balcony.*]

NASTI [*to* SCHMIDT]: Now let him try and surrender the city.

A MAN OF THE PEOPLE [*appearing in the doorway*]: There was no corn in his storehouse.

NASTI: Then he has hidden it at the monastery.

A MAN [*shouting*]: To the monastery! To the monastery!

[*The crowd rushes after him, crying:* 'To the monastery! To the monastery!']

NASTI [*to* SCHMIDT]: Tonight, I shall try to cross the lines.

[*They go out.* HEINRICH *rises, looks around him. He is alone with the* PROPHET. *He sees the* BISHOP, *his eyes wide open, staring at him.*]

HEINRICH: Nasti! [*He tries to enter the palace, but the* BISHOP *stretches out his arm to prevent him.*] I will not enter. Lower your arm – lower your arm. If you are still alive, forgive me. Bitterness is heavy and belongs to the earth. Leave it on earth, and die the lighter. [*The* BISHOP *tries to speak.*] What? [*The* BISHOP *laughs.*] A traitor? I? Of course. They also call me traitor. But explain; how can I betray everybody at once? [*The* BISHOP *is still laughing.*] I loved them. Oh, God! How I loved them. I loved them, but I lied to them. I lied to them by my silence. I held my peace! I held my peace! My lips were tight shut, my teeth clenched. They were dying like flies, and I still held my peace. When they cried for bread, I held out the crucifix. Can you feed a man with the cross? Ah! Lower your arm! We are both guilty. I wanted to share their poverty, suffer their cold, endure their hunger. They died all the same, didn't they? That was a way of betrayal. I made them believe the Church was poor. Now, rage has seized them, and they kill; they are damned; they will never know anything but Hell; first in this world, and tomorrow in the next. [*The* BISHOP *mutters unintelligibly.*] What could I have done? How could I have stopped them? [*He goes to the back, and looks down the street.*] The square is swarming with people; they are hammering on the door of the monastery with benches. The door is solid. It will hold until morning. I can do nothing. Nothing, nothing! Come, close your eyes, die bravely. [*The* BISHOP *drops a key.*] What key is that? What door does it open? A door in the palace! No? The cathedral? Yes? In the sacristy? No? The crypt? ... Is it the door of the crypt? The one that is always closed? Well?

THE BISHOP: Underground. ... Underground.

HEINRICH: Where does it lead? ... Don't tell me! Please God, let him die before he tells me!

THE BISHOP: Outside.

HEINRICH: I refuse to pick it up. [*Pause*] An underground passage leads from the crypt outside the walls. You want me to find Goetz and let him enter Worms by that passage? Never believe it.

THE BISHOP: Two hundred priests. Their lives are in your hands. [*Pause*]

HEINRICH: I understand now why you laughed. It is a rich joke. Thank you, holy Bishop, thank you. The poor will massacre the priests, or Goetz will massacre the poor. Two hundred priests or twenty thousand men, you leave me a fair choice. The question is to know how many men equal a priest. And I have to decide; after all, I belong to the Church. I refuse to pick it up. The priests will go straight to heaven. [*The* BISHOP *dies.*] ... Unless they die like you, with rage in their hearts. Well, it is over with you. Farewell. Forgive him, Lord, as I have forgiven him. I refuse to pick it up. That's enough. No! No! No! [*He picks up the key.*]

THE PROPHET [*rising*]: Oh Lord, let Thy will be done on earth. The world is finished! Finished! Thy will be done on earth!

HEINRICH: Oh Lord, Thou hast cursed Cain and the children of Cain. Thy will be done. Thou hast permitted men to have their hearts torn, their intentions rotted, their actions diseased and stinking; Thy will be done. Oh Lord, Thou hast decreed that my fate should be a traitor's here on earth. Thy will be done. Thy will be done! Thy will be done! [*He goes out.*]

THE PROPHET: Chastise the flesh! Arise, arise. God is there!

[*The lights fade.*]

*

SCENE TWO

The outskirts of GOETZ'S *camp. Night. In the background, the town. An* OFFICER *appears and gazes towards the city. Another* OFFICER *enters immediately behind him.*

SECOND OFFICER: What are you doing?

FIRST OFFICER: Watching the town. One fine day, it might fly away ...

SECOND OFFICER: It won't fly away. We shan't have such luck. [*Turning abruptly*] What's that?

[TWO MEN *appear, carrying a body on a stretcher, covered by a cloth. They are silent. The* FIRST OFFICER *goes to the stretcher, lifts the cover and lets it fall back into place.*]

FIRST OFFICER: To the river. At once!

SECOND OFFICER: Is he ...?

FIRST OFFICER: Black.

[*Pause. The two stretcher-bearers start to go. The sick man groans.*]

SECOND OFFICER: Wait. [*They stop.*]

FIRST OFFICER: What now?

SECOND OFFICER: He is still alive.

FIRST OFFICER: I don't want to know. To the river!

SECOND OFFICER [*to the stretcher-bearers*]: What regiment?

THE STRETCHER-BEARER: Blue Cross.

SECOND OFFICER: What! One of mine! About turn!

FIRST OFFICER: Are you mad? To the river!

SECOND OFFICER: I refuse to let my men be drowned like a litter of kittens.

[*The two officers stare at each other. The stretcher-bearers exchange amused looks, put the dying man down, and wait.*]

FIRST OFFICER: Dead or alive, if we keep him here he'll spread cholera through the entire army.

THIRD OFFICER [*entering*]: If it isn't cholera, it will be blind panic. Hurry! Throw him in the river!

THE STRETCHER-BEARER: He's groaning.

[*Pause. The* SECOND OFFICER *turns towards the stretcher-bearers furiously, draws his dagger, and strikes the body.*]

SECOND OFFICER: That'll stop him groaning. Away! [*The two men go out.*] Three. Three since yesterday.

HERMANN [*entering*]: Four. One has just dropped in the middle of the camp.

SECOND OFFICER: Did the men see him?

HERMANN: In the middle of the camp, I tell you.

THIRD OFFICER: If I were in command, we'd raise the siege this very night.

HERMANN: Agreed. But you aren't in command.

FIRST OFFICER: We must speak to him.

HERMANN: Who do you suggest for the job? [*Silence. They look at each other.*] You will do as he commands.

SECOND OFFICER: Then it's all up with us. If the cholera spares us, we'll get our throats cut by our own men.

HERMANN: Unless he should be the one to die.

FIRST OFFICER: What of? Cholera?

HERMANN: Cholera, or other causes. [*Pause*] I've been told the Archbishop wouldn't be displeased. [*Silence*]

SECOND OFFICER: I couldn't.

FIRST OFFICER: Nor I. He sickens me so much I should be disgusted by the mere idea.

HERMANN: We're not asking you to do anything – except hold your peace and not interfere with others who are less disgusted than you are.

[*Silence.* GOETZ *and* CATHERINE *enter.*]

GOETZ [*entering*]: Have you any news for me? None? Not even that the troops are hungry? That cholera is decimating my ranks? Nothing to ask me? Not even to raise the siege? [*Pause*] Are you all so afraid of me? [*They are silent.*]

CATHERINE: How they stare at you, my jewel. These men don't love you. I shouldn't be surprised if one day we find you on your back with a big knife sticking out of your guts.

GOETZ: Do you love me?

CATHERINE: God, no!

GOETZ: Well, you don't seem to have killed me.

CATHERINE: Not because I haven't wanted to.

GOETZ: I know. You still dream lovely dreams. But I need not fear. The moment I die, you'll be set upon by twenty thousand men. And twenty thousand are rather too many, even for you.

CATHERINE: Better ten thousand than one you detest.

GOETZ: What I like in you is the horror you feel for me. [*To the officers*] When would you like me to raise the siege? Thursday? Tuesday? Sunday? Well, my friends, it won't be Tuesday, Thursday or Sunday. I take the city tonight.

SECOND OFFICER: Tonight?

GOETZ: Tonight. [*Looking towards the town*] There, in the distance, can you see a little blue light? Every night I watch it, and every night, at this moment, it goes out. Look! What did I tell you? I have seen it go out for the hundred and first and last time. Good night; we must kill the thing we love. And there are others ... other lights that disappear. God's blood, there are men who go early to bed because they wish to rise early tomorrow. And there will be no tomorrow. A fine night, eh? Not very much light but swarming with stars; later, the moon will rise. Just the kind of night when nothing happens. They have foreseen everything, accepted everything, even a massacre, but not for tonight. The sky is so pure that it fills them with confidence, this night belongs to them. [*Abruptly*] What power! God, this city is mine, and I give it to Thee. In a moment I will set it on fire and let it blaze to Thy glory! [*To the officers*] A priest has escaped from Worms and says he will help us enter the city. Captain Ulrich is questioning him.

THIRD OFFICER: Hm!

GOETZ: What is it?

THIRD OFFICER: I don't like traitors.

GOETZ: Don't you? Personally, I adore them.

[*An officer enters, pushing the priest guarded by a soldier.*]

HEINRICH [*falling on his knees in front of* GOETZ]: Torture me! Tear off my nails! Skin me alive!

[GOETZ *bursts out laughing.*]

GOETZ [*falling on his knees beside the priest*]: Rip out my guts! Roast me alive! Tear me in pieces! [*He rises.*] Well, that's broken the ice. [*To the captain*] Who is he?

CAPTAIN: Heinrich, a priest from Worms. The one who is supposed to betray the city.

GOETZ: Well?

CAPTAIN: He says he won't tell us any more.

GOETZ [*going to* HEINRICH]: Why?

CAPTAIN: He says he has changed his mind.

THIRD OFFICER: Changed his mind! Holy Jesus! Break his teeth! Smash his jaw!

HEINRICH: Break my teeth! Smash my jaw!

GOETZ: What a lunatic! [*To* HEINRICH] Why did you want to deliver the town to us?

HEINRICH: To save the priests the people want to murder.

GOETZ: And why have you changed your mind?

HEINRICH: I have seen the faces of your mercenaries.

GOETZ: So what?

HEINRICH: They were eloquent.

GOETZ: What did they say?

HEINRICH: That I should precipitate a massacre by trying to prevent a few murders.

GOETZ: You must have seen other soldiers. And you knew they never look very kind-hearted.

HEINRICH: The ones here look much worse than the others.

GOETZ: Pooh! Pooh! All soldiers look alike. What did you expect to find here? Angels?

HEINRICH: Men. And I would have asked those men to spare their fellow men. They would have entered the city having sworn to me to spare the lives of the inhabitants.

GOETZ: You would have taken my word?

HEINRICH: *Your* word? [*He looks at him.*] You are Goetz?

GOETZ: Yes.

HEINRICH: I ... I thought I could trust you.

GOETZ [*surprised*]: Trust my word? [*Pause*] I give it you. [HEINRICH *is silent.*] If you let us into the city, I swear I will spare the lives of the inhabitants.

HEINRICH: You want me to believe you?

GOETZ: Wasn't that your intention?

HEINRICH: Yes. Before I had seen you.

GOETZ [*beginning to laugh*]: Yes, yes, I know. Those who see me, rarely trust my word; I must look far too intelligent to keep it. But listen to me; take me at my word. Just to find out! Merely to find out ... I'm a Christian, after all. If I swore to you on the Bible? Let us go through with the game of blind trust. Isn't it your role as priest to use Good to tempt the wicked?

HEINRICH: Use Good to tempt you? You'd enjoy it far too much!

GOETZ: You understand me. [*He looks at* HEINRICH *with a smile.*] Leave us, all of you.

[*The officers and* CATHERINE *go out.*]

GOETZ [*with a kind of tenderness*]: You are sweating. How you are suffering!

HEINRICH: Not enough! Others suffer, but not I. God has allowed me to be haunted by the suffering of others without ever feeling those sufferings myself. Why are you looking at me?

GOETZ [*still tenderly*]: In my day I had just such a hypocrite's pan. I am looking at you, but I'm sorry for myself. We belong to the same race.

HEINRICH: That's not true! You betrayed your own brother. I shall never betray my own people.

GOETZ: You'll betray them this very night.

HEINRICH: Neither this night nor ever. [*Pause*]

GOETZ [*in a detached voice*]: What will the people do to the priests? Hang them from the butchers' hooks?

HEINRICH [*with a cry*]: Be quiet! [*He recovers himself.*] Those are the horrors of war. I am only a humble priest, unable to prevent them.

GOETZ: Hypocrite! Tonight you have power of life and death over twenty thousand men.

HEINRICH: I refuse to accept that power. It comes from the Devil.

GOETZ: You refuse it, but you possess it all the same. [HEINRICH *tries to escape.*] Hola! What are you doing? If you run away it means you have agreed.

[HEINRICH *returns, looks at* GOETZ *and begins to laugh.*]

HEINRICH: You're right. Whether I kill myself or run away it makes no difference. They are only ways of holding my peace. I am the elect of God.

GOETZ: Why not say rather you have the soul of a rat.

HEINRICH: It's the same thing; an elect is a man the finger of God has driven into a corner. [*Pause*] Oh Lord, why hast Thou elected me?

GOETZ [*gently*]: This is the moment of your agony. I wanted to shorten it for you. Let me help you.

HEINRICH: Help me? You? When God is silent? [*Pause*] Very well, I lied; I am not His elect. Why should I be? Who forced me to leave the city? Who ordered me to come and find you? I elected myself. When I came to ask your mercy for my brothers, I was already sure you would refuse. It wasn't the wickedness in your faces which made me change my mind, it was their reality. I dreamed of doing Evil, and when I saw you all, I understood I was going to do it in fact. Do you know I hate the poor?

GOETZ: Yes, I know.

HEINRICH: Why do they turn away when I stretch out my arms? Why do they suffer always so much more than I could ever suffer? Oh Lord, why hast Thou allowed the common people to exist? Or else, why didst Thou not make of me a monk? In a monastery, I should belong only to Thee. But how can I belong to Thee alone while there are men around me dying of hunger? [*To* GOETZ] I came to deliver them all to you, and I hoped you would exterminate them and let me forget they ever existed.

GOETZ: So?

HEINRICH: So I have changed my mind. You shall never enter the city.

GOETZ: Supposing it were the will of God that you should make us enter? Listen to me; if you hold your tongue, the priests will die this very night; that's certain. But the people? Do you believe they will survive? I shall not raise the siege; within a month, every human creature in Worms will have died of hunger. You don't have to decide between their life or death, but to choose for them between two kinds of death. Gutless coward – choose the swifter way. Do you know what they'll gain by it? If they die tonight before they kill the priests, they will keep their hands clean; everyone will meet again in heaven. If you choose the second way, after the pitiful weeks you leave them, you'll send them, all besmeared with blood, to the depths of Hell. Come now, priest; it was the Devil who whispered to you to spare their earthly lives merely to give them time to damn their souls for ever. [*Pause*] Tell me how to get into the city.

HEINRICH: You are a dead man.

GOETZ: What?

HEINRICH: Your words are dead before they reach my ears, your face is not like those a man can meet in daylight. I know everything you will say, I can foresee all your movements. You are my own creation, and your thoughts come only at my bidding. I am dreaming, the world is dead, and the very air is full of sleep.

GOETZ: In that case, I am dreaming too. I can see your future so clearly, your present bores me. All we need to know

now is which one of the two is living in the dream of the other.

HEINRICH: I never left the city! I never left it! We are acting in front of painted cloths. Come along, fine actor, give me my cues to speak. Do you know your own part? Mine is to say no. No! No! No! No! You say nothing? This is no more than an ordinary temptation, without much truth about it. What should I be doing in Goetz's camp? [*He gestures towards the city.*] If only those lights could extinguish themselves! What is the town doing over there, since I am within its walls! [*Pause*] A temptation exists, but I do not know where it should be. [*To* GOETZ] What I do know clearly is that I am going to see the Devil; when he is preparing to pull faces at me, the entertainment begins with a fantasy.

GOETZ: Have you seen the Devil already?

HEINRICH: More often than you have seen your own mother.

GOETZ: Do I look like him?

HEINRICH: You, my poor man? You are the jester.

GOETZ: What jester?

HEINRICH: There always has to be a jester. His role is to contradict me. [*Pause*] I have won.

GOETZ: What?

HEINRICH: I have won. The last lamp has gone out; the devilish phantom of Worms has disappeared. We can relax. You will disappear in your turn, and this ridiculous temptation will come to an end. Darkness, darkness and night over the whole world. What peace.

GOETZ: Go on, priest, go on. I remember everything you are still going to say. A year ago ... Oh yes, brother mine, I remember. How you would like to bring all that darkness into your head. How often I have desired it myself.

HEINRICH [*in a murmur*]: Where shall I be when I wake up?

GOETZ [*laughing suddenly*]: You are awake, you cheater, and you know it. Everything is real. Look at me, touch me, I am flesh and blood. Look, the moon is rising, your devilish city emerges from the shadows; look at the town. Is it a mirage? Come now! It is real stone, those are real ramparts, it is a real town with real inhabitants. And you – you are a real traitor.

HEINRICH: A man is a traitor only when he betrays. You can do what you like, I shall never betray the city.

GOETZ: A man will betray when he is already a traitor; you will betray the city. Come now, father, you are a traitor *already*; two paths lie before you, and you pretend you can follow both at the same time. So you are playing a double game, you are thinking in two languages. The suffering of the poor, you call that a test in Church Latin, and in common German you translate it as iniquity. What more can happen to you if you help me enter the city? You will become the traitor you already are, that is all. A traitor who betrays is a traitor who accepts himself.

HEINRICH: How do you know this if your words aren't dictated by my will?

GOETZ: Because I am a traitor too. [*Pause*] I have already covered the road you still have to take, and yet look at me; don't I seem to be flourishing?

HEINRICH: You are flourishing because you have followed your nature. All bastards betray, it's a well-known fact. But I am not a bastard.

GOETZ [*hesitates before striking him, then controls himself*]: Usually those who call me bastard never do it twice.

HEINRICH: Bastard!

GOETZ: Father! Little father! Do try and be serious. Don't force me to cut off your ears; it won't help in the least because I shall leave you your tongue. [*Abruptly, he kisses* HEINRICH.] Hail, little brother! Welcome to bastardy! You are a bastard too! To engender you, the Clergy coupled with Misery; what joyless fornication. [*Pause*] Naturally, bastards betray, what else should they do? I have been two people all my life; my mother gave herself to a cut-throat, and I am composed of two halves which do not fit together; each of those halves shrinks in horror from the other. Do you believe you are better served? A half-priest added to a half-peasant, that doesn't add up to a whole man. We *are* nothing and we *have* nothing. Every infant born in wedlock can inherit the earth without paying. But not you, and not I. Since the day of my birth, I have only seen the world through the keyhole; it's a fine little egg, neatly packed, where everyone fits the place God has assigned to him. But I give you my word we are not inside that world. We are outcasts! Reject this world that refuses you. Turn to Evil; you will see how light-hearted you feel. [*An* OFFICER *enters.*] What do you want?

THE OFFICER: An envoy from the Archbishop.

GOETZ: Send him in.

THE OFFICER: He brings news; the enemy leaves seven thousand dead. The rout is complete.

GOETZ: My brother? [*The* OFFICER *tries to whisper in his ear.*] Keep your distance. Speak out.

THE OFFICER: Conrad is dead.

[*From this moment,* HEINRICH *watches* GOETZ *closely.*]

GOETZ: I see. Has his body been found?

THE OFFICER: Yes.

GOETZ: In what condition? Answer me!

THE OFFICER: Disfigured.

GOETZ: A sword-cut?

THE OFFICER: Wolves.

GOETZ: Wolves? Are there wolves?

THE OFFICER: The forest of Arnheim ...

GOETZ: Very well. Let me once settle this little matter, and I march against Arnheim with the entire army. I will tear the hide from every wolf in the forest of Arnheim ... Get out. [*The* OFFICER *goes. Pause*] Dead without absolution; the wolves have eaten his face, but as you see, I am still smiling.

HEINRICH [*softly*]: Why did you betray him?

GOETZ: Because I like things to be clear-cut. Priest, I created myself, I was only a bastard by birth, but the fair title of fratricide I owe to no one but myself. [*Pause*] It belongs to me now, to me alone.

HEINRICH: What belongs to you?

GOETZ: The castle of Heidenstamm. They are finished, the Heidenstamms, finished, liquidated. I contain them all in myself, from Alberic the founder of the family, down to Conrad, the last male heir to the line. Look at me well, priest, I am a family mausoleum. Why are you laughing?

HEINRICH: I thought I should be the only one to see the Devil tonight, and now I know there will be two of us.

GOETZ: I don't give a damn for the Devil! He receives our souls, but it isn't he who condemns them. I refuse to deal with anyone but God. Monsters and saints exist only because of God. God sees me, priest, He knows I killed my brother, and His heart bleeds. Yes, indeed, oh Lord, I killed him. And what can You do against me? I have committed the worst of crimes, and the God of justice is powerless to punish me; He damned me more than fifteen years ago. There – enough for one day. This is a holiday. I'm going to have a drink.

HEINRICH [*going to him*]: Here. [*He brings a key out of his pocket, and holds it out to* GOETZ.]

GOETZ: What is this?

HEINRICH: A key.

GOETZ: What key?

HEINRICH: The key to Worms.

GOETZ: Enough for one day, I said. A brother – good God. You don't bury a brother every day; I have the right to give myself a holiday until tomorrow.

HEINRICH [*bearing down on him*]: Coward!

GOETZ [*stopping*]: If I take this key, I burn everything.

HEINRICH: At the bottom of this ravine, there is a white boulder. At its base, hidden among brushwood, there is an opening. Follow the passage underground, and you will find a door you can open with this.

GOETZ: How they'll love you, your little brothers of the poor! How they're going to bless you!

HEINRICH: That's no concern of mine any more. I am lost, by my own choice. But I leave my poor in your hands, bastard. Now, it is you who have to choose.

GOETZ: You said just now you had only to see my face ...

HEINRICH: I had not seen it closely enough.

GOETZ: And what do you see in it at this moment?

HEINRICH: That you hate yourself.

GOETZ: It's true, but don't put your trust in that! I have hated myself for fifteen years. So what? Don't you understand that Evil is my reason for living? Give me that key. [*He takes it.*]

Well, little priest, you will have lied to the very end. You thought you had found a way of disguising your treason from yourself. But once and for all, you have finally betrayed. You have betrayed Conrad.

HEINRICH: Conrad?

GOETZ: Don't be afraid. You resemble me so closely that I took you for myself. [*He goes.*]

CURTAIN

*

SCENE THREE

GOETZ's *tent.*

Through the opening we can see the town in the distance, bathed in moonlight.

HERMANN *enters and tries to hide under the camp bed. His head and body disappear, but we can still see his enormous behind.* CATHERINE *enters, goes to him and gives him a kick. He rises, terrified. She springs away from him, laughing.*

HERMANN: If you call out ...

CATHERINE: If I call out, you'll be discovered, and Goetz will skin you alive. Much better talk this over. What are you going to do to him?

HERMANN: What you should have done, harlot, if you had had any blood in your veins – what you should have done a very long time ago. Get out of here! Go for a walk, and thank God that a man has taken on your job for you. D'you hear?

CATHERINE: What will become of me, if he dies? The whole camp will fall upon me.

HERMANN: We'll help you escape.

CATHERINE: Will you give me some money?

HERMANN: A little.

CATHERINE: Give me my dowry and I'll enter a convent.

HERMANN [*laughing*]: A convent – you! If you want to live in a community, why not enter a brothel; with the talent you have between your thighs you'd earn a fortune in no time. Make up your mind. I only ask you to hold your tongue.

CATHERINE: My silence – you can count on that; at all events, I shan't betray you. When it comes to cutting his throat ... that depends.

HERMANN: Depends on what?

CATHERINE: We don't share the same interests, pretty captain. A man's honour can be redeemed at the point of a knife. But a woman – he has made me a whore, and I am much more difficult to redeem. [*Pause*] Tonight the city will be taken. The war is over, everyone can go home. When he arrives, in a few minutes, I'll ask him what he intends to do with me. If he keeps me ...

HERMANN: Goetz keep you? You're mad. What do you expect him to do with you?

CATHERINE: If he keeps me you shan't touch him.

HERMANN: And if he sends you away?

CATHERINE: Then he is all yours. If I cry out: 'You asked for it', come out of hiding, and he'll be at your mercy.

HERMANN: I don't want my whole plan to depend on a question of f ...

CATHERINE [*who for a moment or two has been watching outside*]: Then fall on your knees and ask him to forgive you. Here he is.

[HERMANN *runs to hide himself.* CATHERINE *begins to laugh.*]

GOETZ [*entering*]: Why are you laughing?

CATHERINE: I was laughing at my dreams; I saw you lying dead with a knife in your back. [*Pause*] So, he's talked?

GOETZ: Who?

CATHERINE: The priest.

GOETZ: What priest? Oh yes! Yes, of course.

CATHERINE: And you'll do it tonight?

GOETZ: What's it to do with you? Take off my boots. [*She takes them off.*] Conrad is dead.

CATHERINE: I know. Everyone in the camp knows.

GOETZ: Give me a drink. We must celebrate. [*She pours his wine.*] Drink too.

CATHERINE: I don't want to drink.

GOETZ: God's blood! Drink, this is a holiday.

CATHERINE: A fine holiday that begins with a murder and ends with a holocaust.

GOETZ: The finest holiday in my life. Tomorrow, I leave for my estates.

CATHERINE [*surprised*]: So soon?

GOETZ: So soon! For thirty years I have dreamed of this moment. I shall not wait a single extra day. [CATHERINE *seems upset.*] Don't you feel well?

CATHERINE [*pulling herself together*]: It was hearing you talk of *your* estates while Conrad's body is still warm.

GOETZ: They have been mine in secret for thirty years. [*He raises his glass.*] I drink to my lands and my belongings. Drink with me. [*She raises her glass in silence.*] Say: to your estates!

CATHERINE: No.

GOETZ: Why not, bitch?

CATHERINE: Because they are not yours. Will you cease to be a bastard because you assassinated your brother? [GOETZ *begins to laugh, aims a blow at her, which she dodges and sinks on the bed, laughing.*] Estates pass from father to son by inheritance.

GOETZ: I'd have to be paid a good price before I'd accept them that way. Nothing belongs to me except what I take. Come, drink the toast or I'll have to lose my temper.

CATHERINE: To your estates! To your castles!

GOETZ: And may there be legions of outraged phantoms in the corridors at night.

CATHERINE: That's true, mountebank. What would you do without an audience? I drink to your phantoms. [*Pause*] So, my sweetheart, nothing belongs to you except what you take by force?

GOETZ: Nothing.

CATHERINE: But, apart from your manors and your domains, you possess a priceless treasure, though you don't seem aware of it.

GOETZ: What treasure?

CATHERINE: Me, my darling, me. Didn't you take me by force? [*Pause*] What are you going to do with me? Tell me.

GOETZ [*looking at her reflectively*]: I'll take you with me.

CATHERINE: You will? Why? [*She takes a hesitating step towards him.*] To set a harlot at the head of a noble house?

GOETZ: To set a harlot in the bed of my noble mother.

CATHERINE: And if I refuse? If I didn't want to go with you?

GOETZ: I sincerely hope you don't want to come.

CATHERINE: Ah! You'll carry me away by force. That's better. I should have been ashamed to follow you of my own free will. [*Pause*] Why do you always want to force what might perhaps be given you with good grace?

GOETZ: To make sure I should be given it with bad grace. [*He goes to her.*] Look at me, Catherine. What are you hiding?

CATHERINE [*quickly*]: I? Nothing!

GOETZ: For some time now I've seen a change in you. You still hate me passionately, don't you?

CATHERINE: Yes, indeed, with all my strength!

GOETZ: You still have dreams that somebody will kill me?

CATHERINE: Every night.

GOETZ: You aren't forgetting it was I who ruined and soiled you?

CATHERINE: I can never forget.

GOETZ: And you submit to my caresses with repugnance?

CATHERINE: They make me shudder.

GOETZ: Good. If you ever get the idea of wanting to come to my arms, I shall drive you away immediately.

CATHERINE: But ...

GOETZ: I shall accept nothing ever again, not even favours from a woman.

CATHERINE: Why?

GOETZ: Because I have been given enough. For twenty years, everything has been given to me most graciously, down to the very air I breathe; a bastard has to kiss the hand that feeds him. Oh! How I am going to give back in my turn! How generous I am going to be!

FRANZ [*entering*]: The Envoy of his Excellency is here.

GOETZ: Send him in.

THE BANKER [*entering*]: I am Foucre.

GOETZ: I am Goetz. This is Catherine.

THE BANKER: Delighted to meet so great a captain.

GOETZ: And I to salute so rich a banker.

THE BANKER: I am the bearer of three excellent pieces of news.

GOETZ: The Archbishop is victorious, my brother is dead, his lands and fortune belong to me. Isn't that it?

THE BANKER: Exactly. And so, I ...

GOETZ: Let us celebrate. D'you want a drink?

THE BANKER: Unfortunately, my stomach won't take wine. I ...

GOETZ: Do you want this handsome slut? She is yours.

THE BANKER: I shouldn't know what to do with her. I am too old.

GOETZ: Poor Catherine, he doesn't want you. [*To the* BANKER] Do you prefer young boys? You'll find one in your tent this evening.

THE BANKER: No, no! No boys! Most definitely, no boys! I ...

GOETZ: What d'you say to a heavy dragoon? I have one six feet high, covered with hair ... a real gorilla.

THE BANKER: No! No! Most certainly not ...

GOETZ: In that case, we'd better give you glory. [*He shouts*] Franz! [FRANZ *appears.*] Franz, take this gentleman for a tour of the camp, and see that the soldiers shout, 'Long live the banker!' tossing their caps in the air. [FRANZ *exits.*]

THE BANKER: I am much obliged, but I wanted to talk to you immediately. In private.

GOETZ [*surprised*]: What have you been doing ever since you came in? [*Nodding towards* CATHERINE] Oh! That one ... She's a domestic animal; speak without fear.

THE BANKER: His Eminence has always been most peaceful, and you know your late brother was responsible for beginning this war ...

GOETZ: My brother! [*Violently*] If that old idiot hadn't driven him to extremes ...

THE BANKER: Sir, sir ...

GOETZ: Yes. Forget what I just said, but you'll oblige me by leaving my brother out of this. After all, I am wearing his mourning.

THE BANKER: Therefore, his Eminence has decided to mark the return of peace by measures of exceptional clemency.

GOETZ: Bravo! Is he opening the prisons?

THE BANKER: The prisons? Good heavens, no!

GOETZ: Does he wish me to remit the punishments of any soldiers I have sentenced myself?

THE BANKER: He desires it, certainly. But the amnesty he envisages has a much more general character. He wants to extend it to his subjects in Worms.

GOETZ: Ah! Ah!

THE BANKER: He has decided not to punish them for a momentary deflection.

GOETZ: It seems an excellent idea.

THE BANKER: Can we be in agreement so soon?

GOETZ: Entirely in agreement. [*The* BANKER *rubs his hands.*]

THE BANKER: Well, well, that's perfect; you are a reasonable man. When are you thinking of lifting the siege?

GOETZ: Tomorrow it will be all over.

THE BANKER: Tomorrow – that seems a little too soon. His Eminence desires to enter into negotiations with the besieged. If your army remains under their walls a few days longer, the ambassadors will find their task facilitated.

GOETZ: I see. And who is going to negotiate?

THE BANKER: I am.

GOETZ: When?

THE BANKER: Tomorrow.

GOETZ: Impossible.

THE BANKER: Why?

GOETZ: Catherine! Shall we tell him?

CATHERINE: Of course, my jewel.

GOETZ: Then you tell him. I dare not, it will cause him too much pain.

CATHERINE: Tomorrow, banker, all those people will be dead.

THE BANKER: Dead?

GOETZ: All of them.

THE BANKER: All dead?

GOETZ: All dead. This very night. You see this key? It opens the city. One hour from now, the massacre begins.

THE BANKER: Everyone? Including the rich?

GOETZ: Including the rich.

THE BANKER: But you approved the Archbishop's clemency ...

GOETZ: I still approve it. He has been sinned against, and he is a priest; two reasons to forgive the offenders. But why should I forgive them? The inhabitants of Worms haven't sinned against me. No, no, I am a soldier, therefore I must do a soldier's work. I will kill them according to my office, and the Archbishop will forgive them, according to his own.

[*Pause. Then the* BANKER *begins to laugh.* CATHERINE *laughs, then* GOETZ *begins to laugh too.*]

THE BANKER [*laughing*]: I see you like laughing.

GOETZ [*laughing*]: It's the only thing I do like.

CATHERINE: He's very witty, isn't he?

THE BANKER: Most witty. He's managing this business excellently.

GOETZ: What business?

THE BANKER: For thirty years, I have run my business on one principle; that interest directs the world. When they come to see me, men justify their behaviour by citing the most exalted motives. I listen to them with one ear, and I say to myself – find where their interest lies.

GOETZ: And when you found it?

THE BANKER: Then we could talk.

GOETZ: Have you found mine?

THE BANKER: Oh, really!

GOETZ: What is it?

THE BANKER: Gently, gently. You belong to a category which is very difficult to handle. With a man like you, one has to proceed one step at a time.

GOETZ: What category?

THE BANKER: You are an idealist.

GOETZ: What the hell's that?

THE BANKER: I divide men into three categories; those who have a great deal of money, those who have none at all, and those who have only a little. The first want to keep what they have; their interest is to maintain order; the second want to take what they have not; their interest is to destroy the present order and establish another which would be profitable to them. Both of them are realists, men with whom one can come to an understanding. The third want to overturn our social order to take what they have not, while at the same time making quite sure no one takes away what they already have. Therefore, they conserve in fact what they destroy in desire, or rather, they destroy in fact what they are only pretending to conserve. Those people are idealists.

GOETZ: How are we to cure the poor?

THE BANKER: By transferring them to another social level. If you were to make them rich, they would defend the established order.

GOETZ: Then you should make me rich. What do you offer?

THE BANKER: Conrad's possessions.

GOETZ: You've already given them to me.

THE BANKER: Exactly. Only remember you owe them to the bounty of his Eminence.

GOETZ: Believe me, I shall not forget. What else?

THE BANKER: Your brother was in debt.

GOETZ: The poor fellow! [*He crosses himself, and sobs nervously.*]

THE BANKER: What's the matter?

GOETZ: Very little; a touch of family feeling. So, you say he was in debt.

THE BANKER: We could pay those debts for you.

GOETZ: That is not to my interest because I had no intention of acknowledging them. You should address yourself to his creditors.

THE BANKER: An annual income of one thousand ducats?

GOETZ: And my soldiers? Supposing they refuse to go away empty-handed?

THE BANKER: Another thousand to distribute among them. Is it enough.

GOETZ: Far too much.

THE BANKER: Then we are agreed?

GOETZ: No.

THE BANKER: Two thousand ducats annually? Three thousand? I can go no higher.

GOETZ: Who is asking you to?

THE BANKER: Then what do you want?

GOETZ: To take and destroy the city.

THE BANKER: I don't mind if you take it, but good heavens, why should you want to destroy it?

GOETZ: Because everyone else wants me to spare it.

THE BANKER [*stunned*]: I must have been wrong ...

GOETZ: Indeed yes! You couldn't discover my interest! Come now, what can it be? Think! Think hard! But hurry; you must find it within the next hour; if between now and then you haven't discovered what strings make the marionette move, I shall have you dragged through the streets, and you will see the fires of destruction lighted one after the other.

THE BANKER: You are betraying the Archbishop's trust.

GOETZ: Betrayal? Trust? You are all the same, you realists; when you don't know what else to say, you have to borrow the language of us idealists.

THE BANKER: If you destroy the city, you will never possess your brother's lands.

GOETZ: Keep them! My interest, banker, was to have them and to live there. But I'm not so sure men act only by their interest. Keep the lands, I tell you, and let his Eminence stuff them up. I sacrificed my brother to the Archbishop, and now you're expecting me to spare twenty thousand lives? I shall offer the inhabitants of Worms to the spirit of Conrad; they will be roasted alive in his honour. As for the domain of Heidenstamm, let the Archbishop go into retirement there, if he likes, and spend the rest of his days studying agriculture; he will have need to, for I intend to ruin him this very night. [*Pause*] Franz! [FRANZ *appears.*] Take this venerable realist, see that all honours are shown him, and when he is under his tent, make sure that his hands and feet are securely tied.

THE BANKER: No! No, no, no!

GOETZ: What's the matter?

THE BANKER: I suffer from atrocious rheumatism. Your cords will be worse than murder. Shall I give you my word of honour not to leave my tent?

GOETZ: Your word of honour? It's in your interest to give it, but quite soon, it will be in your interest not to keep it. Take him away, Franz, and see that the knots are pulled tight.

[FRANZ *and the* BANKER *go out. Immediately there are cries of* 'Hurrah for the banker' *at first near at hand, then dying away in the distance.*]

GOETZ: 'Hurrah for the banker!' [*He bursts out laughing.*] Farewell the estates! Farewell the fields and rivers! Farewell to the castle!

CATHERINE [*laughing*]: Farewell the estates! Farewell to the castle! Farewell the family portraits!

GOETZ: Don't regret anything! We would have been bored to death. [*Pause*] The old fool! [*Pause*] Ah! He shouldn't have defied me.

CATHERINE: Are you very unhappy?

GOETZ: Hold your tongue! [*Pause*] To do Evil must in the long run harm everyone. Including the one who sets it in motion.

CATHERINE [*timidly*]: Supposing you didn't take the city?

GOETZ: If I don't take it, you'll be mistress of a castle.

CATHERINE: I wasn't thinking of that.

GOETZ: Of course not. You needn't worry; I shall take it.

CATHERINE: But why?

GOETZ: Because it is evil.

CATHERINE: Why should you want to do evil?

GOETZ: Because Good has been done already.

CATHERINE: By whom?

GOETZ: By God the Father. I have to invent. [*He calls*] Ho, there! Captain Schoene. At once. [GOETZ *stands at the entrance to the tent, and looks out into the night.*]

CATHERINE: What are you looking at?

GOETZ: The city. [*Pause*] I was wondering if that night there was a moon too ...

CATHERINE: When? Where? ...

GOETZ: Last year, when I was about to take Halle. It was a night very like this one. I stood at the entrance to my tent and watched the belfry rising above the ramparts. In the morning, we took the place by assault. [*He comes back to her.*] In any case, I'll get out of here before it begins to stink. Saddle and spurs and away.

CATHERINE: You ... you're going away?

GOETZ: Tomorrow, before midday, without a word to anyone.

CATHERINE: And me?

GOETZ: You? Stop your nose and pray that the wind doesn't blow from that quarter. [*The* CAPTAIN *enters.*] Two thousand men under arms; the Wolfmar and Ulrich regiments. Have them ready to follow me in half an hour. The rest of the army stand to arms. Put out all lights, and make your preparations in silence. [*The* CAPTAIN *goes out. Until the end of the act, there are muffled sounds of preparation.*] So you see, sweetheart, you will never be mistress of a castle.

CATHERINE: I'm afraid not.

GOETZ: Very disappointed?

CATHERINE: I never believed it would happen.

GOETZ: Why not?

CATHERINE: Because I know you.

GOETZ [*violently*]: You know me? [*He stops short and laughs.*] After all, I suppose I am predictable too. [*Pause*] You must have your own ideas about how to manage me; you watch me, you look at me ...

CATHERINE: A cat can look at a king.

GOETZ: Yes, but the cat sees the king with the head of a cat. What do you see me as? A cat? A mackerel? A cod? [*He looks at her.*] Come on the bed.

CATHERINE: No.

GOETZ: I said come. I want to make love.

CATHERINE: I've never seen you so pressing. [*He takes her by the shoulders.*] Nor so depressed. What's the matter?

GOETZ: It's the Goetz with the fish-eyes who is beckoning me. He and I want to get together. Besides, agony of mind can be resolved in physical love.

CATHERINE: Your mind is in agony?

GOETZ: Yes. [*He goes to sit on the bed, turning his back on the hidden officer.*] Come here!

[CATHERINE *goes to him, and pulling him up roughly, sits down in his place.*]

CATHERINE: I'm here, yes, and I belong to you. First of all, tell me what will happen to me?

GOETZ: When?

CATHERINE: After tomorrow.

GOETZ: How the hell should I know? Whatever you like.

CATHERINE: In other words, I am to become a harlot.

GOETZ: I'd say it was the best solution, wouldn't you?

CATHERINE: Supposing I don't want that?

GOETZ: Find some poor specimen to marry you.

CATHERINE: What will you do – after tomorrow?

GOETZ: Stick to my soldiering. They tell me the Hussites are nervous; I'll go and give them a few knocks.

CATHERINE: Take me with you.

GOETZ: What for?

CATHERINE: There will be times when you'll need a woman; when the moon will be shining, and you'll have to take a city; a night when you'll be in anguish, and you'll want to make love.

GOETZ: All women are alike. My men will bring them to me in dozens if the urge should ever take me.

CATHERINE [*abruptly*]: I won't have it!

GOETZ: You won't have what?

CATHERINE: I can be twenty women, a hundred, if you like, all the other women in one. Take me up behind you. I weigh very little, your horse will never feel me. I want to be your brothel! [*She presses herself to him.*]

GOETZ: What's come over you? [*Pause. He looks at her. Then suddenly*] Get out. I'm ashamed of you.

CATHERINE [*imploringly*]: Goetz!

GOETZ: I won't allow you to look at me like that. You must be completely rotten to dare love me after all I have done to you.

CATHERINE [*crying out*]: I don't love you! I swear I don't love you! Even if I did, you'd never know of my love! What difference does it make if someone loves you, provided they never tell you!

GOETZ: What business have I to be loved? If you love me, you'll be the one who enjoys it. Get out of here, you bitch! I won't let anyone profit at my expense.

CATHERINE [*crying out*]: Goetz! Goetz! Don't send me away! I have no one in the world.

[GOETZ *tries to throw her out of the tent. She clings to his hands.*]

GOETZ: Will you get out of here!

CATHERINE: You asked for it. Goetz! You asked for it! [HERMANN *rushes out of hiding, and springs forward, his dagger raised.*] Look behind you! Ah!

GOETZ [*turns round and catches* HERMANN'S *wrist*]: Franz! [*Two soldiers enter. He laughs.*] At any rate, I have managed to drive someone to desperation.

HERMANN [*to* CATHERINE]: Rotten bitch! Filthy traitor!

GOETZ [*to* CATHERINE]: You knew about this? I like that better; I like that very much better. [*He strokes her chin.*] Take him away ... I'll decide what to do with him later.

[*The soldiers go out, taking* HERMANN. *Pause*]

CATHERINE: What will you do to him?

GOETZ: I can never be angry with anyone who tries to kill me. I understand their point of view too well. I'll have him put in the cellar, that's all – like the fat barrel of beer he is.

CATHERINE: And what will you do to me?

GOETZ: Yes. I suppose I'll have to punish you too.

CATHERINE: There's no real obligation.

GOETZ: Oh yes, there is. [*Pause*] A great many of my soldiers have dry lips when they see you. I'll make them a present of you. Afterwards, if you're still alive, we'll choose a nice squint-eyed, pock-marked bastard, and the priest of Worms can marry you to him.

CATHERINE: I don't believe you.

GOETZ: No?

CATHERINE: No. You're not ... You'll never do it. I'm quite sure! I'm absolutely sure!

GOETZ: I'll never do it? [*He calls*] Franz! Franz! [FRANZ *appears with two soldiers.*] Take away the bride, Franz!

FRANZ: What bride?

GOETZ: Catherine. You'll marry her first to everyone, with tremendous pomp. Afterwards ... [NASTI *enters, goes to* GOETZ *and strikes him on the ear.*] Hey, peasant, what are you doing?

NASTI: I struck you on the ear.

GOETZ: I felt it. [*Holding him*] Who are you?

NASTI: The baker, Nasti.

GOETZ [*to the soldiers*]: Is this Nasti?

THE SOLDIERS: Yes. That's him.

GOETZ: A fine prize, by God.

NASTI: I am not your prize. I surrendered myself.

GOETZ: Just as you like; it comes to the same thing. God is overwhelming me with presents today. [*He looks at* NASTI.] So this is the famous Nasti, lord of every beggar in Germany. You are exactly as I imagined you; as depressing as virtue.

NASTI: Don't believe I am virtuous, Our sons will be virtuous if we shed enough blood to give them the right to become so.

GOETZ: I see. You are a prophet.

NASTI: In common with all men.

GOETZ: Indeed? Then I am a prophet too?

NASTI: All words are God's witness; all words reveal all to all people.

GOETZ: The devil! I'll have to be careful of what I say.

NASTI: To what end? You cannot prevent yourself revealing everything.

GOETZ: I see. Very well, answer my questions and try not to tell me quite everything, or we'll never come to the end. So, you are Nasti, prophet and baker.

NASTI: I am.

GOETZ: I heard you were in Worms.

NASTI: I escaped.

GOETZ: This evening?

NASTI: Yes.

GOETZ: To talk to me?

NASTI: To find reinforcements and attack you in the rear.

GOETZ: Excellent idea. What made you change your mind?

NASTI: As I was crossing the camp, I heard a traitor had betrayed the city.

GOETZ: You must have had a bad quarter of an hour.

NASTI: Yes. Very bad.

GOETZ: So then?

NASTI: I was sitting on a rock behind your tent. I saw the tent light up and shadows move. At that moment, I received an order to go to you and speak to you.

GOETZ: Who gave you that order?

NASTI: Who do you suppose it could be?

GOETZ: Who indeed? Happy man; you receive your orders, and you know who has given them to you. Curiously enough, I've had my orders too – to take and burn Worms. But I never know who commands me. [*Pause*] Was it God who commanded you to strike me over the ear?

NASTI: Yes.

GOETZ: Why?

NASTI: I don't know. Perhaps to loosen the wax which prevents you from hearing.

GOETZ: You have forfeited your own head in consequence. Did God tell you that too?

NASTI: God had no need to tell me. I have always known how I should finish.

GOETZ: Of course – you're a prophet. I had forgotten.

NASTI: I don't need to be a prophet; we others, we have only two ways to die. Those who are resigned, die of hunger. Those who are not resigned, die by hanging. At twelve years old, you already know if you are resigned or not.

GOETZ: Fine. Well, now you should kneel before me.

NASTI: What for?

GOETZ: To beg for mercy, I suppose. Didn't God command you to do that? [FRANZ *puts on his boots.*]

NASTI: No. You have no mercy, and God has none either. Why should I ask for your mercy when, by morning, I shall have no mercy for others?

GOETZ [*rising*]: Then what the hell did you come here for?

NASTI: To open your eyes, my brother.

GOETZ: Oh, night of wonders! All is in motion, God walks upon earth, my tent is a heaven filled with shooting stars, and here is the fairest of all; Nasti, the prophet from the bakehouse, sent here to open my eyes. Who would have believed that heaven and earth would make so much ado for one town of twenty thousand inhabitants? By the way, baker, who assures you that you aren't a victim of the Devil?

NASTI: When the sun dazzles your eyes, who proves to you that it isn't night?

GOETZ: At night, when you dream of the sun, who proves to you that it isn't morning? Supposing I had seen God too? Eh? Ah! It would be sunlight against sunlight. [*Pause*] I hold you all in my hands, all of you; this harlot who wanted to kill me, the envoy of the Archbishop, and you, the king of the beggars. God's finger has revealed the conspiracy, the guilty are unmasked; better still, it was one of God's ministers who brought me the keys of the city with His compliments.

NASTI [*in a changed voice, imperative and brusque*]: One of God's ministers? Which one?

GOETZ: What do you care since you are about to die? Come now, admit that God is on my side.

NASTI: On your side? No. You are not a man of God. At the very most you are His lackey.

GOETZ: How do you know?

NASTI: The real men of God destroy or construct. You merely conserve.

GOETZ: I?

NASTI: You bring about disorder. And disorder is the best servant of the established power. You weakened the entire order of chivalry the day you betrayed Conrad, and you'll be weakening the burghers the day you destroy Worms. Who will profit by your action? The rulers. You serve the rulers, Goetz, and you will serve them whatever you do; all destruction confuses; weakens the weak, enriches the rich, increases the power of the powerful.

GOETZ: Therefore, I am doing the opposite of what I intend?

[*Ironically*] Happily, God has sent you to enlighten me. What do you propose?

NASTI: A new alliance.

GOETZ: Oh! A new betrayal? Isn't that charming; at all events, I am used to it. It won't be much change for me. But if I must ally myself not with the burghers, the knights or the princes, I don't quite see who I am to join with.

NASTI: Take the city, massacre the rich and the priests, give everything to the poor, raise an army of peasants and drive out the Archbishop. Tomorrow the whole country will march behind you.

GOETZ [*amazed*]: You expect me to join the poor?

NASTI: With the people, yes! With the plebs from the city, and the peasants from the fields.

GOETZ: What an extraordinary idea!

NASTI: They are your natural allies. If you want to destroy in good earnest, raze the palaces and cathedrals erected by the power of Satan, shatter the obscene pagan statues, burn the thousands of books which spread diabolic knowledge, suppress gold and silver, come to us, be one of us. Without us, you are turning in a circle, you hurt no one but yourself. With us, you will become the scourge of God.

GOETZ: What will you do to the burghers?

NASTI: Take their possessions from them, to cover the naked and feed the hungry.

GOETZ: The priests?

NASTI: Send them back to Rome.

GOETZ: And the nobles?

NASTI: Cut off their heads.

GOETZ: And when we have driven out the Archbishop?

NASTI: It will be time to build the city of God.

GOETZ: On what foundations?

NASTI: That all men are brothers and equals. That all are in God and God is in all; the Holy Ghost speaks through all mouths, all men are priests and prophets, all men can baptize, conduct marriages, interpret God's will and remit sins; all men live openly on earth in the sight of men, and solitarily within their souls in the sight of God.

GOETZ: It won't be easy to laugh in your city.

NASTI: Can you laugh at what you love? Our one law will be the law of Love.

GOETZ: And what shall I be within your city?

NASTI: The equal of all men.

GOETZ: Supposing I don't want to be your equal?

NASTI: The equal of all men or the lackey of the princes. Choose.

GOETZ: Your proposition is very honest, baker. Only, you see, the people bore me to death; they hate everything I enjoy.

NASTI: What do you enjoy?

GOETZ: Everything you want to destroy; statues, luxury, war.

NASTI: The moon is not yours, my poor misguided friend, and you've been fighting all your life so that the nobles may possess it.

GOETZ [*deeply and sincerely*]: But I love the nobles.

NASTI: You? You assassinate them.

GOETZ: Nonsense! I assassinate them a little, from time to time, because their wives are fertile, and they make ten more for every one I may have killed. But I won't let you hang them all. Why should I help you put out the sun, and extinguish the earthly torches? We should create a polar night.

NASTI: Then you will go on being nothing but a useless uproar.

GOETZ: Useless, yes. Useless to men. But what do I care for men? God hears me, it is God I am deafening, and that is enough for me, for He is the only enemy worthy of my talents. There is only one God, the phantoms and myself. It is God I shall crucify this night, through you, and through twenty thousand men, because His suffering is infinite, and it renders infinite those whom He causes to suffer. This city will go up in flames. God knows that. At this moment, He is afraid, I can feel it; I feel His eyes on my hands, His breath on my hair, the tears of His angels. He is saying to Himself, 'Perhaps Goetz will not dare ...' exactly as if He were no more than a man. Weep, weep, pretty angels; I shall dare. In a few moments, I will march in His fear and

His anger. The city shall blaze; the soul of the Lord is a corridor of mirrors, the fire will see itself reflected in a thousand glasses. Then, I shall know that I am a monster in all purity. [*To* FRANZ] Bring me my sword.

NASTI [*in a changed voice*]: Spare the poor. The Archbishop is rich, you can amuse yourself ruining him, but the poor, Goetz, it isn't amusing to make them suffer.

GOETZ: No, indeed, it is far from amusing.

NASTI: Well, then?

GOETZ: I have my orders, I have my orders too.

NASTI: I implore you on my knees.

GOETZ: I thought you were forbidden to pray to men.

NASTI: Nothing is forbidden when it is a question of saving lives.

GOETZ: It looks to me, prophet, as though God had led you into an ambush. [NASTI *shrugs his shoulders.*] You know what is going to happen to you?

NASTI: Torture and hanging, yes. I told you I have always known.

GOETZ: Torture and hanging ... Hanging and torture ... how monotonous. The boring part of Evil is that one grows accustomed to it – you need genius to invent. Tonight, I don't feel at all inspired.

CATHERINE: Let him have a confessor.

GOETZ: A ...

CATHERINE: You cannot let him die without absolution.

GOETZ: Nasti! There's the stroke of genius. Of course, my dear man, of course you shall have a confessor! It's my duty as a Christian. Besides, I have a surprise for you. [*To* FRANZ] Go and fetch the priest ... [*To* NASTI] There's an act such as I love; with facets. Is it good? Is it evil? The understanding is confused.

NASTI: No Papist is going to soil me.

GOETZ: You'll be tortured until you confess your sins – it will be entirely for your own good.

[*Enter* HEINRICH.]

HEINRICH: You have done me all the harm you could. Leave me in peace.

GOETZ: What was he doing?

FRANZ: Sitting in the dark, shaking his head.

HEINRICH: What do you want of me?

GOETZ: Put you to work at your profession. You must marry this woman immediately. As for this man, you must give him the last sacraments.

HEINRICH: This man? ... [*He sees* NASTI.] Ah! ...

GOETZ [*pretending to be surprised*]: You know each other?

NASTI: Is this the minister of God who gave you the key?

HEINRICH: No! No, no!

GOETZ: Priest, aren't you ashamed to lie?

HEINRICH: Nasti! [NASTI *will not look at him.*] I couldn't let them massacre the priests. [NASTI *is silent.* HEINRICH *goes to him.*] Tell me, could I let them be killed? [*Pause. He turns and goes to* GOETZ.] Well? Why must I hear his confession?

GOETZ: Because he is going to be hanged.

HEINRICH: Then do it quickly! Hang him quickly! And find him another confessor.

GOETZ: It must be you, or no one.

HEINRICH: Then it will be no one. [*He turns to go.*]

GOETZ: Hey! Hey! [HEINRICH *stops.*] Can you allow him to die without confession?

HEINRICH [*returning slowly*]: No, jester, no; you are right. I cannot do that. [*To* NASTI] Kneel. [*Pause*] You will not? My brother, my sins do not reflect on the Church, and it is in the name of the Church that I can remit your sins. Would you like me to make public confession? [*To the others*] I betrayed my city out of spite and malice; I deserve to be scorned by everyone. Spit in my face, and let there be no more of this. [NASTI *does not move.*] You – soldier – spit!

FRANZ [*gaily, to* GOETZ]: Shall I spit?

GOETZ [*equally gaily*]: Spit, my boy, and do a good job while you're at it!

[FRANZ *spits at* HEINRICH.]

HEINRICH: Now all is over. Heinrich is dead of shame. The priest remains. An anonymous priest; and it is before him that you must kneel. [*After a moment of waiting, he strikes* NASTI *suddenly.*] Murderer! I must be mad to humiliate myself before you when everything that happened was your fault!

NASTI: My fault!

HEINRICH: Yes! Yes! You are responsible. You wanted to be a prophet, and here you are defeated, a prisoner waiting for the hangman, and all those who trusted you are going to die. All! All of them! Ha! Ha! You pretended you knew how to love the poor, and I didn't know the way; well, you see; you have done them more harm than I have.

NASTI: More than you, you excrement! [*He throws himself on* HEINRICH. *They are dragged apart.*] Who betrayed the city? You or I?

HEINRICH: I did! I did! But I should never have done it if you hadn't murdered the Bishop.

NASTI: God commanded me to strike him because he was starving the poor.

HEINRICH: God, indeed? How simple it all is; then God commanded me to betray the poor because the poor wanted to murder the monks!

NASTI: God *cannot* command anyone to betray the poor – God is always on their side.

HEINRICH: If He is on their side why do their revolts always fail? Why has He permitted your revolt to finish in despair today? Come along, answer me! Answer! Why don't you answer me? You cannot?

GOETZ: This is the moment. This is the agony. This is the sweat in drops of blood. There! There! Agony is refreshing. How gentle you look; I see your face, and I feel that twenty thousand men are about to die. I love you. [*He kisses* NASTI *on the mouth.*] Come now, brother, the last word has not been spoken; I decided I would take Worms, but if God is on your side, something may happen to prevent me.

NASTI [*in a low voice, with conviction*]: Something will happen.

HEINRICH [*crying out*]: Nothing. Nothing at all! Nothing will happen. It would be much too unjust. If God had to work a miracle, why should He not have done it before I became a traitor? Why should He damn me if He were going to save you?

[*An* OFFICER *enters. All are startled.*]

THE OFFICER: All is ready. The troops are drawn up at the edge of the ravine, behind the chariots.

GOETZ: So soon? [*Pause*] Tell Captain Ulrich I am coming.

[*The* OFFICER *goes out.* GOETZ *sinks into a chair.*]

CATHERINE: There's your miracle, sweetheart. [GOETZ *passes his hand over his face.*] Go! Pillage and slaughter! And so, good night.

GOETZ [*with a weariness which changes into a simulated exaltation*]: This is the moment of farewell. When I return, I shall be covered with blood and my tent will be empty. Pity, I had grown accustomed to you. [*To* NASTI *and* HEINRICH] You will spend the night together, like a couple of lovers. [*To* HEINRICH] Be sure and hold his hand tenderly while they are ripping his guts out. [*To* FRANZ, *pointing to* NASTI] If he agrees to confess, stop the torture immediately; as soon as he has been absolved, string him up. [*As if suddenly remembering the existence of* CATHERINE] Ah, the bride! Franz, you will assemble the stable boys, and introduce them to Madame. Let them do what they like, short of killing her.

CATHERINE [*suddenly throwing herself at his feet*]: Goetz! Pity! Pity! Not that! Not that horror! Pity!

GOETZ [*recoiling, astonished*]: You were so proud and confident just now ... You didn't believe me?

CATHERINE: No, Goetz, I didn't believe you.

GOETZ: To tell you the truth, I didn't believe in it myself. You only believe in Evil *afterwards.* [*She clings to his knees.*] Franz, take her away. [FRANZ *pulls her away and throws her on the bed.*] There we are. I have forgotten nothing ... No! I really believe I have forgotten nothing. [*Pause*] Still no miracle; I'm beginning to think God is giving me a free hand. Thank you, oh Lord, thank you very much. Thank you for the women violated, the children impaled; the men decapitated. [*Pause*] If only I wanted to talk! I know so much, you dirty hypocrite. Listen, Nasti, I'm going to give you the answer; *God is making use of me.* You saw how it was tonight; well, He sent His angels down to save me.

HEINRICH: His angels?

GOETZ: All of you. Catherine is very certainly an angel. So are you, so is the banker. [*Returning to* NASTI] What about this key? Did I ask God to send me this key? I didn't even suspect its existence; but God had to send one of His ministers to place it in my hands. Naturally, you all know what He desires. That I should spare His priests and rescue His nuns. Therefore, He tempts me, very gently, making opportunities without compromising Himself. If I am caught, He has the right to disown me; after all, I could easily throw this key into the ravine.

NASTI: Yes, you could. You can still.

GOETZ: No, indeed, my angel. You know perfectly well that I cannot.

NASTI: Why not?

GOETZ: Because I cannot be other than myself. Listen, I am going to take a nice little blood bath to oblige the good Lord. But when it is all over, He will stop His nose and cry that that wasn't at all what He wanted. Do you really not want it, oh Lord? Then there is still time to prevent me. I don't ask for the heavens to fall on my head; a mere expectoration would suffice; let me slip in a man's slime, break my thigh, and that would be enough for one day. No? Fine, fine. I don't insist. Look, Nasti, look at this key; a key is a fine thing, a key is a useful thing. And look at these hands. There's workmanship. We should all praise the Lord for giving us hands. Then, if you hold a key in your hands, that cannot be wicked; let us praise the Lord for all the hands holding keys at this moment in all the countries of the world. But as for what the hand does with the key, the Lord declines responsibility, that doesn't concern Him at all, the poor fellow. Yes, Lord, You are completely innocent; how can You conceive nothingness, You who are fullness itself? Your presence is light, and changes all into light; how are You to know the half-light of my heart? And Your infinite understanding? How can it enter my reasons without bursting them asunder? Hatred and weakness, violence, death, displeasure, all that proceeds from man alone; it is my only empire, and I am alone within it; what happens within me is attributable to me alone. There – there – I take everything on myself, and I shall never utter one complaint. On the Day of Judgement, silence, shut lips; I am far too proud. I shall let myself be damned without uttering a word. But doesn't it embarrass You a little, Lord, a very little, to have to damn the man who does Your work for You? I am going, I am going, the men are waiting, the good little key is dragging me along – it wants to go home to its beloved keyhole. [*In the tent opening, he turns back.*] Do any of you know my equal? I am the man who makes the All-Powerful uneasy. Through me, God is disgusted by Himself. There are twenty thousand nobles, thirty bishops, fifteen kings, we've had three emperors, a pope, and an anti-pope. But can you offer me another Goetz? Sometimes, I imagine Hell an empty desert waiting for me alone. Farewell. [*He turns to go.* HEINRICH *bursts out laughing.*] What's the matter?

HEINRICH: But Hell is a public convenience! [GOETZ *stops and looks at him. To the others*] This is the strangest of all visionaries; a man who believes he alone is doing Evil. Every night the soil of Germany is illuminated by living torches; tonight, as on every night, cities are going up in flames by dozens, and the captains who command the sackings don't make nearly so much fuss about it. They kill, on weekdays, and then, on Sundays, go to confession, humbly. But this man takes himself for the Devil incarnate, because he is carrying out his duties as a soldier. [*To* GOETZ] If you are the Devil, jester, who am I, I who pretended to love the poor, and delivered them up to the mercy of your soldiers?

[GOETZ *stares at* HEINRICH, *almost fascinated, during this speech. When it is over, he shakes himself.*]

GOETZ: What are you demanding? The right to be damned as well? I grant it you. Hell is wide enough for me not to meet you there.

HEINRICH: And the others?

GOETZ: What others?

HEINRICH: All the others. All those who haven't the luck to kill, but desire it with their whole hearts.

GOETZ: My wickedness is not their wickedness; they do

Evil as a luxury, or out of interest; I do Evil for Evil's sake.

HEINRICH: What do reasons matter if it is proved that a man can *only* do Evil?

GOETZ: Has it been proved?

HEINRICH: Yes, jester, it has been proved.

GOETZ: By whom?

HEINRICH: By God Himself. God has made it impossible for man to do Good on this earth.

GOETZ: Impossible?

HEINRICH: Completely impossible. Love is impossible! Justice is impossible! Why don't you try and love your neighbour? You can tell me afterwards what success you have.

GOETZ: Why shouldn't I love my neighbour if I should so decide?

HEINRICH: Because if only one man should hate another, it would be sufficient for hatred to spread from one to another and overwhelm mankind.

GOETZ [*continuing*]: This man here loves the poor.

HEINRICH: Yet he lied to them most cunningly, he excited their lowest passions and encouraged them to murder an old man. [*Pause*] What could I do? Tell me what could I have done? I was innocent, and yet the crime fell upon my shoulders, like a thief attacking in the night. Where was the Good then, eh? Where was the least Evil? [*Pause*] You are taking a great deal of trouble for nothing, you vaunter of the ways of vice! If you want to deserve Hell, you need only remain in bed. The world itself is iniquity; if you accept the world, you are equally iniquitous. If you should try and change it, then you become an executioner. [*He laughs.*] The stench of the world puts out the stars.

GOETZ: Then all are damned?

HEINRICH: Ah no, not all! [*Pause*] I have my faith, oh God, I have my faith. I shall not fall into the sin of despair. I am infected to the very marrow, but I know Thou wilt deliver me if Thou hast so decided. [*To* GOETZ] We are all equally guilty, bastard, we are all equally deserving of hell-fire, but the Lord forgives us when it pleases Him to forgive.

GOETZ: He will never forgive me against my will.

HEINRICH: Miserable wretch, how can you struggle against His mercy? How can you exhaust His infinite patience? He will take you up between His fingers if He pleases, raise you to the level of His paradise; with the tip of His finger He will make you overflow with His goodwill, and you will find yourself becoming good despite yourself. Go! Burn Worms. Go to pillage, go to massacre – you're wasting your time; one of these days you'll wake up in Purgatory like everyone else.

GOETZ: Then everyone is doing Evil?

HEINRICH: Everyone.

GOETZ: And no one in the world has ever done only Good?

HEINRICH: No one.

GOETZ: Perfect. [*He re-enters the tent.*] I will make a wager with you that I shall.

HEINRICH: Shall what?

GOETZ: Live righteously. Will you take the bet?

HEINRICH [*shrugging his shoulders*]: No, bastard, I will wager nothing at all.

GOETZ: You are wrong; you tell me Good is impossible – therefore I wager I will live righteously; it is obviously the best way to live alone. I was a criminal – I will reform. I turn my coat, and become a saint.

HEINRICH: Who will be the judge?

GOETZ: You yourself. In a year and a day from now. You have only to make your bet.

HEINRICH: You fool, if you wager on such a thing you have lost your bet in advance. You will be righteous merely to win a bet.

GOETZ: Very well. Here are the dice. If I win, Evil triumphs. If I lose – ah! If I lose, I am not in the smallest doubt as to what I shall do. Well? Who plays against me? Nasti?

NASTI: No.

GOETZ: Why not?

NASTI: It is wrong.

GOETZ: Of course it is wrong. What else did you expect? Come along, baker, I am still wicked for the moment.

NASTI: If you want to live righteously, you need only make up your mind. That is all.

GOETZ: I want to drive the Lord into a corner. This time it is yes, or no. If He lets me win, the city burns, and His responsibility is established. Come now, play; if God is with you, you must never fear. You dare not, coward? You prefer to be hanged? Who will dare?

CATHERINE: I will.

GOETZ: You, Catherine? [*He looks at her.*] Why not? [*He hands her the dice.*] Throw.

CATHERINE [*throwing the dice*]: A two and a one. [*She shudders.*] You'll find it very difficult to lose.

GOETZ: Who said I want to lose? [*He puts the dice back in the box.*] Lord – this time You're caught. The moment has come to show Your hand. [*He throws the dice.*]

CATHERINE: One and one ... You've lost!

GOETZ: I submit to the will of God. Farewell, Catherine.

CATHERINE: Kiss me. [*They kiss.*] Farewell, Goetz.

GOETZ: Take this purse, and go where you please. [*To* FRANZ] Franz, take word to Captain Ulrich to send the men to rest. Nasti – you will return to the city, there is still time to prevent a panic. If you open the gates at dawn, if the priests leave Worms safe and sound, and place themselves under my protection, I will lift the siege at noon. Agreed?

NASTI: Agreed.

GOETZ: Have you recovered your faith, prophet?

NASTI: I never lost it.

GOETZ: Fortunate man!

HEINRICH: You can restore their liberty, you can give them back their life and hope. But me, you dog, me who you forced into betrayal, can you ever restore my purity?

GOETZ: It's up to you to find it again. After all, there was no real harm done.

HEINRICH: What matters whether the harm was done? It is my intention that matters. I'll follow you, yes, I'll follow, step by step, night and day; you can rely on me to judge your actions. You can rest happy, in a year and a day, wherever you may be, I shall meet you at the time and place appointed.

GOETZ: Here is the dawn. How cold it is. The dawn and absolute Good have entered my tent, and none of us is any happier; this woman weeps, that man hates me bitterly; it feels like the aftermath of disaster. Perhaps Good is a disaster ... At all events, it doesn't concern me now. I don't have to judge it, but to do it. Farewell. [*He goes out.* CATHERINE *begins to laugh.*]

CATHERINE [*laughing till the tears roll down her cheeks*]: He let me beat him! I saw! I saw! He let me beat him – but he had to cheat first!

CURTAIN

Act 2

SCENE FOUR

The castle of Heidenstamm.

FIRST PEASANT: Shouting their heads off, in there.

KARL: It's the barons; they're mad with rage.

FIRST PEASANT: Supposing he loses his nerve and gives in?

KARL: Don't worry; he's as stubborn as a mule. Careful – hide. He's coming.

GOETZ [*to* KARL]: Dear brother, will you bring us some wine? Three cups will suffice – I shall not drink myself. Do this for the love of me, brother.

KARL: For the love of you, brother, I will.

[GOETZ *goes out. The peasants come out of hiding, laughing and slapping their thighs.*]

THE PEASANTS: Brother – little brother! Baby brother! Take that! Take that for the love of me! [*They buffet each other joyously, laughing all the while.*]

KARL [*arranging glasses on a tray*]: All the servants are his brothers. He says he loves us, he coaxes us, and kisses us too, sometimes. Yesterday he decided to wash my feet. The kind lord, the good brother. Pah! [*He spits.*] That word burns my lips, and I spit every time I have to say it. He'll be hanged because he called me brother, and when they put the rope round his neck, I'll kiss him on the lips and say: 'Good night, little brother. Die now for the love of me.' [*He goes out, carrying the tray with the glasses.*]

FIRST PEASANT: There goes a real man. No one ever gets round him.

SECOND PEASANT: They say he knows how to read, too.

FIRST PEASANT: Holy Virgin!

KARL [*returning*]: These are your orders. Visit everyone on the estates of Nossak and Schulheim. Spread the news in the smallest hamlet: 'Goetz is giving the peasants the lands of Heidenstamm.' Give them time to digest that, and then say: 'If that bastard, that son-of-a-bitch has given his lands away, why does the high and mighty lord of Schulheim not give you his?' Work them all up, work them up into a rage, spread trouble everywhere. Go. [*They go out.*] Goetz, my darling brother, you'll see how I'll spoil your good works. Give away your lands, give them all away: one day you'll be sorry you didn't fall dead before you gave them away. [*He laughs.*] For love of you! Every day I dress you, and undress you. I see your navel, your toes, your behind, and you expect me to love you. I'll give you love. Conrad was hard and brutal, but his insults offended me less than your kindnesses. [*Enter* NASTI] What do you want?

NASTI: Goetz sent for me.

KARL: Nasti!

NASTI [*recognizing him*]: It's you!

KARL: So you know Goetz? Charming friendship.

NASTI: Don't worry about that. [*Pause*] I know what you're planning, Karl! You'd do much better to lay low and wait quietly for my orders.

KARL: The country takes no orders from the town.

NASTI: If you try and pull this dirty trick, I'll have you hanged.

KARL: Take care the one hanged doesn't turn out to be you. To begin with, what are you doing here? It's very odd. You've come to talk to Goetz, and you tell us not to revolt! Who's to say you haven't been bribed!

NASTI: Who's to say you haven't been bribed to make the revolt break out prematurely and so have it crushed the more easily?

KARL: Here comes Goetz.

[GOETZ *enters, backing away from the barons* SCHULHEIM, NOSSAK, *and* REITSCHEL, *who are pressing around him, shouting.*]

NOSSAK: You don't give a damn for the peasants: what you want is our necks.

SCHULHEIM: You're hoping to use our blood to wipe away the bitcheries of your mother.

NOSSAK: You're digging the graves of all the German nobility.

GOETZ: My brothers, my very dear brothers, I don't even know what you are talking about.

REITSCHEL: You don't know that this gesture of yours will put the match to the powder? That our peasants will be mad with rage if we don't immediately give them our lands, our possessions, down to our very shirts, and then our blessing on top of everything?

SCHULHEIM: I suppose you don't know they'll come and besiege us in our homes?

REITSCHEL: That if we accept it means our ruin, and if we refuse it means our death?

NOSSAK: You don't know any of that?

GOETZ: My very dear brothers ...

SCHULHEIM: No speeches! Will you renounce your plans? Answer yes or no.

GOETZ: My very dear brothers, forgive me: I say no.

SCHULHEIM: You're an assassin!

GOETZ: Yes, my brother, like everyone.

SCHULHEIM: A bastard!

GOETZ: Yes; like Jesus Christ.

SCHULHEIM: You sack of excrement! You encumberer of the earth! [*He drives his fist into* GOETZ'S *face.* GOETZ *staggers, then recovers, and advances on* SCHULHEIM. *They all shrink away. Suddenly, he flings himself full length on the ground.*]

GOETZ: Help, angels, help! Help me to overcome myself! [*He trembles all over.*] I won't strike him. I'll cut off my right hand if it wants to strike him. [*He writhes about on the ground.* SCHULHEIM *kicks him.*] Roses, rain of roses, gentle caresses. How God loves me. I accept everything. [*He rises.*] I'm a dog of a bastard, a receptacle of filth, a traitor, pray for me.

SCHULHEIM [*striking him*]: Will you give up your plan?

GOETZ: Don't strike me. You will soil yourself.

REITSCHEL [*threateningly*]: Will you give it up?

GOETZ: Oh Lord, deliver me from the abominable desire to laugh!

SCHULHEIM: Good God!

REITSCHEL: Come away. We're wasting our time.

[*The barons go out, and* GOETZ *becomes aware of the two men.*]

GOETZ [*joyfully*]: Hail, Nasti! All hail, my brother. I am happy to see you again. Two months ago, in front of Worms, you offered me an alliance with the people. Today I can accept. Wait: I must speak. I have good news for you. Before doing Good, I told myself I had to know what it was, and I considered for a long time. Well, Nasti, now I know what Good must be. It is love, of course: but the fact is that men don't love one another, and what is it that prevents them? Inequality of conditions, servitude and misery. Therefore, these things must be suppressed. Up till now, we are in agreement, are we not? Nothing surprising about that; I have profited by your lessons. Yes, Nasti, I have thought of you a great deal, these last weeks. Only, you want to postpone the kingdom of God: I am much more cunning; I have found a way to establish it now, at least in a single corner of the world – here. Firstly: I give up my lands to the peasants. Secondly: on this very land, I shall organize the first truly Christian community: all equal! Ah, Nasti, I am a captain: I engage the battle of Good and I think I shall be able to win it at once, and without shedding blood. Will you help me? You know how to speak to the poor. We two will be able to construct a Paradise, for the Lord Himself has chosen me to efface our original sin. Listen, I have found a name for my Utopia: I shall call it the City of the Sun. What's the matter? You're as stubborn as a mule! Ah, you killjoy! What else have you found to reproach me with?

NASTI: Keep your lands for yourself.

GOETZ: Keep my lands! And it's you, Nasti, who is asking this? I expected everything, excepting that.

NASTI: Keep them. If you want to help us, don't do anything, and above all, don't interfere.

GOETZ: Then you, too, believe that the peasants will revolt?

NASTI: I don't believe it, I know.

GOETZ: I might have known this would happen. I should have foreseen that I should outrage your narrow, prejudiced soul. Those swine just now, and you, at this moment – I must be very right, or you wouldn't all be protesting so loudly. You are only encouraging me! I'll give them all away, these lands of mine. How happy I shall be to give them away! Good shall be done in spite of you all.

NASTI: Who asked you to give them away?

GOETZ: I know I have to give them away.

NASTI: But who asked you?

GOETZ: I know, I tell you. I see my way as clearly as I see you. The Lord has visited His light upon me.

NASTI: When God is silent, you can make Him say whatever you please.

GOETZ: Ah! Admirable prophet! Thirty thousand peasants are dying of hunger, I ruin myself to relieve their misery, and you can only tell me God forbids that I should save them.

NASTI: You – save the poor? You can only corrupt them.

GOETZ: Then who will save them?

NASTI: Don't concern yourself with the poor: they will save themselves.

GOETZ: Then what will become of me, if you take away my means of doing Good?

NASTI: You have plenty to do. Administer your fortune, and watch it grow. That's a task to fill a lifetime.

GOETZ: Then to please you I have to become a wicked rich man?

NASTI: No rich man is wicked. He is rich. That is all.

GOETZ: Nasti, I am one of you.

NASTI: No.

GOETZ: Have I not been poor all my life?

NASTI: There are two kinds of poor – those who are poor in company and those who are poor alone. The first are the real poor, the others are only the rich who've been unlucky.

GOETZ: And the rich who have given away their possessions – they aren't poor either, I suppose.

NASTI: No, they are merely no longer rich.

GOETZ: Then I was beaten in advance. Shame on you, Nasti, you condemn a Christian soul without appeal. [*He walks up and down in agitation.*] However proud those petty lords may be who hate me, you are even prouder, and I should find it less difficult to join their caste than to join yours. Patience! Thanks to Thee, oh Lord, I shall love them without return. My love will break down the walls of your intractable soul: it will disarm the peevishness of the poor. I love you, Nasti, I love you all.

NASTI [*more gently*]: If you love us, give up your plan.

GOETZ: No.

NASTI [*in a changed voice, more urgently*]: Listen. I must have seven years.

GOETZ: To do what?

NASTI: In seven years we shall be ready to begin the holy war. Not before. If you plunge the peasants into this brawl today, I don't give them more than a week. What you will have destroyed in eight days, will need more than half a century to reconstruct.

KARL: My lord, the peasants are here.

NASTI: Send them away, Goetz. [GOETZ *is silent.*] Listen, if you really wish to help us, there is a way.

GOETZ [*to* KARL]: Ask them to wait, my brother. [KARL *goes out.*] What do you propose?

NASTI: Keep your lands.

GOETZ: That depends.

NASTI: If you keep them, they can serve as a place of refuge, and a place of assembly. I shall establish myself in one of your villages. From here, my orders will radiate over Germany; from here, in seven years, will go out the signal for war. You can render us inestimable service. Well?

GOETZ: The answer is no.

NASTI: You refuse?

GOETZ: I cannot do Good in instalments. Haven't you understood, Nasti? Thanks to me, before the year is out, happiness, love, and virtue will reign over ten thousand acres of this land. On my domains I wish to build the City of the Sun, and you want me to turn it into a hiding-place for murderers.

NASTI: Good has to be served like a soldier, Goetz, and what soldier can win a war by himself alone? Begin by being modest.

GOETZ: I will not be modest. As humble as you please, but

never modest. Modesty is the virtue of the half-hearted. [*Pause*] Why should I help you prepare your war? God has forbidden us to shed blood, and you want to make Germany a holocaust? I will not be your accomplice.

NASTI: You refuse to shed blood? Then, give away your lands, give away your castle, and you'll see if this land of ours does not begin to bleed.

GOETZ: Germany will not bleed. Good cannot engender Evil.

NASTI: Good does not engender Evil, true; therefore, because your mad generosity provokes a massacre, what you are doing cannot be Good.

GOETZ: Can it be Good to perpetuate the sufferings of the poor?

NASTI: I ask for seven years.

GOETZ: And for those who die before then? Those who have spent their lives in hatred and fear will die in despair.

NASTI: God will receive their souls.

GOETZ: Seven years! And then in seven years will come seven years of war, and then seven years of repentance because we shall have to build up our ruins again. Who knows what will follow after: a new war, perhaps, and a new repentance, and new prophets who will ask for seven more years of patience. Charlatan! Will you make them wait till the Day of Judgement? I tell you Good is possible, every day, at every hour, at this very moment. I shall be the man who lives by Good alone. Heinrich told me: 'It would be enough for two men to hate each other for hatred, from one to another, to spread throughout the world.' And I tell you, it suffices for one man to love all men with undivided love for that love to spread from one to another throughout humanity.

NASTI: And you will be that man?

GOETZ: Yes, with God's help, I will be that man. I know that Good is much more difficult than Evil. Evil was only myself, but Good is the whole world. I am not afraid. We must bring new warmth to the world, and I will be that warmth. God has commanded me to shine, and I will shine. I will bleed light. I am a burning coal, the breath of God enflames me, and I am consuming alive. Nasti, I am infected with

Good, and my malady must prove contagious. I shall be witness, martyr, and temptation.

NASTI: Impostor!

GOETZ: You shall not shake my resolution! I see, I know, the way is clear. I shall prophesy!

NASTI: False prophet – instrument of the Devil! You are he who says: I shall do what I think right, though the world perish.

GOETZ: The false prophet and the instrument of the Devil is he who says: Let the world perish, and I will then see if Good is possible.

NASTI: Goetz, if you stand in my way, I will destroy you.

GOETZ: Could you kill me, Nasti?

NASTI: Yes, if you stand in my way.

GOETZ: I could not kill you. Love is now my lot. I am going to give away my lands.

CURTAIN

*

SCENE FIVE

Before the portal of a village church. Two benches are under the porch. On one of them is a drum, on the other, a flute. GOETZ *enters, disguised as a monk, followed by* NASTI.

GOETZ [*calling*]: Hola! Ho! Not a soul within thirty leagues: they've all gone to ground. My bounty has descended upon them like a disaster. The fools! [*He rounds on* NASTI.] Why are you following me?

NASTI: To be present at your failure.

GOETZ: There will be no failure. Today I lay the first stone of my city. They are in the cellars, I suppose. But patience. Let me only capture half a dozen, and you'll see if I don't know how to win them over. [*Cries, music of fifes*] What is this? [*Enter a procession of* PEASANTS, *half-drunk, carrying a plaster saint shoulder high on a litter.*] You seem very gay. Are you celebrating the gracious gift of your former lord?

A PEASANT: God forbid, holy father.

GOETZ: I am no monk. [*He throws back his hood.*]

THE PEASANTS: Goetz! [*They recoil, frightened. Some of them cross themselves.*]

GOETZ: Goetz, yes, Goetz, the bogy, Goetz the bugbear! Goetz the Attila who gave away his lands for Christian charity. Do I seem so redoubtable? Come, I wish to speak to you. [*Pause*] Well? What are you waiting for? Come here! [*Silence from the peasants. In a more imperious tone*] Who's in command?

AN OLD MAN [*unwillingly*]: I am.

GOETZ: Come here.

[*The* OLD MAN *moves out from the group and goes to him. The* PEASANTS *watch them in silence.*]

GOETZ: Tell me, I saw sacks of grain in the castle barns. Haven't you understood? No more taxes, no more tithes.

THE OLD MAN: For a little while longer, we leave everything as it should be.

GOETZ: Why?

THE OLD MAN: To see what happens.

GOETZ: Very well. The grain will rot. [*Pause*] What do you think of your new estates?

THE OLD MAN: Don't let us discuss it, my lord.

GOETZ: I am no longer your lord. Call me brother. Understand?

THE OLD MAN: Yes, my lord.

GOETZ: Your brother, I tell you.

THE OLD MAN: Oh no. Not that, no.

GOETZ: I ord ... I beg you.

THE OLD MAN: You can be my brother as much as you like, but I shall never be yours. Each one to his station, my lord.

GOETZ: Never mind! You'll grow used to it. [*Pointing to the flute and the drum*] What are those?

THE OLD MAN: A flute and a drum.

GOETZ: Who plays them?

THE OLD MAN: Monks.

GOETZ: There are monks here?

THE OLD MAN: Brother Tetzel has arrived from Worms with two minor friars. They have to come to sell indulgences.

GOETZ [*bitterly*]: So that is why you seem so gay? [*Abruptly*] The devil! I won't have such mummery here. [*Silence*] Those indulgences are worthless. Do you believe God gerrymanders His forgiveness? [*Pause*] If I were still your master and commanded you to drive these three scoundrels away, would you do it?

THE OLD MAN: Yes, I would.

GOETZ: Well, for the last time, it is your master who commands you ...

THE OLD MAN: You aren't our master any more.

GOETZ: Go away: you are too old. [*He pushes the* OLD MAN *away, leaps up on to a step, and addresses the crowd.*] Have you even wondered why I made you a gift of all my lands? [*Pointing to a peasant*] Answer me.

THE PEASANT: Don't know.

GOETZ [*to a woman*]: Do you?

THE WOMAN [*hesitating*]: Maybe ... maybe because you wanted to make us happy.

GOETZ: Well answered! Yes, that was what I wanted. But you see, happiness is only a means to an end. What do you expect to do with your happiness?

THE WOMAN [*frightened*]: With happiness? First, we've got to have it.

GOETZ: You will be happy, never fear. What will you do with it?

THE WOMAN: Never thought about it. Don't even know what it is.

GOETZ: I have thought about it for you. [*Pause*] You know that God commands us to love one another. Only, you see, up till now it was impossible. Even yesterday, my brothers, you were much too unhappy for anyone to dream of asking you for love. Well, I wanted you all to be without excuse. I am going to make you big and fat, and you will love your neighbours; by heaven, I insist that you love everyone. I give up the command of your bodies, but I have come to guide your souls, for God has visited His light upon me. I am the architect, and you will be my workmen; all for all, the tools and the lands in common. No more poor men, no more rich men, no more laws except the law of love. We shall be an example to all Germany. What do you say, lads, shall we give it a trial? [*Silence*] I am not displeased to see you frightened in the beginning; nothing is more reassuring than a good old devil. But the angels, my brothers! It's the angels who are suspect. [*The crowd smiles, sighs, and begins to stir.*] At last! At last you are smiling at me!

THE CROWD: Here they are! Here they are!

GOETZ [*turns round, sees* TETZEL, *and says bitterly*]: The Devil fly away with the monks!

[*The two minor friars pick up their instruments. A table is brought and set down on the top step.* TETZEL *lays his rolls of parchment on the table.*]

TETZEL: Well, now, little fathers! Come along! Nearer! Nearer! I've not been eating garlic! [*They all laugh.*] How's things in these parts? Is the land good?

THE PEASANTS: Not too bad.

TETZEL: And the wives? Just as unbearable?

THE PEASANTS: You know how it is. Like everywhere else.

TETZEL: You mustn't complain; they protect you against the Devil because they are bigger bitches than he is. [*The crowd laughs.*] Ah, my little friends, that's not what we're here for; we're going to talk about serious things! Music! [*Drum and fife*] Work all the time, is all very fine and large, but sometimes, a man leans on his hoe, looks away into the distance, and says to himself: 'What's going to happen to me after I die?' It's not enough to have a nice little grave, with plenty of flowers: a man's soul doesn't live in the tomb. Then where will the soul go? Down to hell? [*Drum*] Or up to Heaven? [*Flute*] Good people, you can be quite sure the good Lord has asked Himself that question. He is so worried about you, the good Lord, that He doesn't even sleep any more. You, over there, what's your name?

THE PEASANT: Peter.

TETZEL: Tell me, Peter, I expect you take a drop too much from time to time? Come along, don't lie to me!

THE PEASANT: It does happen.

TETZEL: And the wife? You beat her sometimes?

THE PEASANT: When I've been drinking.

TETZEL: And yet you fear God?

THE PEASANT: Oh yes, father!

TETZEL: And the Holy Virgin? Do you love her well?

THE PEASANT: More than my own mother.

TETZEL: Then see how embarrassed the good Lord is. 'That good man is not very wicked, He says to Himself. And I don't want to hurt him very much. Nevertheless, he has sinned, and I must punish him.'

THE PEASANT [*desolate*]: Alas!

TETZEL: But wait a moment. Luckily, there are the Saints! Each one of them has deserved Paradise a hundred thousand times, but what good is that since they can only enter once, each one of them? Then what does the good Lord say to Himself? He says: 'Those hundred thousand entrances that haven't been used, we mustn't waste them, and I'm going to distribute them to those who haven't deserved them. That good Peter, if he buys an indulgence from Brother Tetzel, will enter into Paradise with one of the invitation cards signed by good St Martin.' Well? Well? Wasn't that a good idea? [*Acclamations*] Come along, Peter, bring out your purse. My brothers, God is offering him an incredible bargain. Paradise for only half a ducat. Where is the curmudgeon, where is the miser who won't give half a ducat for his eternal life? [*He takes a coin from* PETER.] Thank you. Go home, and sin no more. Who buys? Look, here is a special bargain. When you give this little note to your own priest, he has to grant you absolution from any mortal sin of your own choosing. Isn't that true, father?

THE PARISH PRIEST: Quite true.

TETZEL: D'you see this? [*He brandishes a parchment.*] Ah, this, my brothers, is a special dainty from the good Lord! These indulgences have all been specially drawn up for people who have members of their family still in Purgatory. If you lay out the necessary, all your late relations will spread their wings and fly to Heaven. The price is two crowns per person transferred: the transfer is immediate. Who buys? Who buys? You there – who have you lost?

THE PEASANT: My mother.

TETZEL: Your mother? Is that all? At your age, have you only lost your mother?

THE PEASANT [*hesitating*]: Well, I did have an uncle ...

TETZEL: And you'd leave your poor uncle in Purgatory? Come along, come along! Count out four crowns. [*He takes them, and holds them out above the alms-box.*] Attention, good people, attention. When the coins fall, the souls will fly away. [*He drops the coins into the box. Flourish from the flute*] One! [*Another flourish on the flute*] And two! There they go! There they go! They are flying over your heads: two lovely pure white butterflies! [*Flute*] We'll meet you in heaven! We'll meet you in heaven! Please pray for us and give our respects to the Saints. Come on, friends, a good hand for the little darlings. [*Applause*] Who's next? [*The peasants surge round him.*] For your wife and your grandmother? For your sister? [*Flute ... flute*] Pay up! Pay up!

GOETZ: Stand back! [*Murmurs from the crowd*]

TETZEL [*to the* PARISH PRIEST]: Who's that?

THE PRIEST: Their former lord. Nothing to fear.

GOETZ: Fools, who believe yourselves quit with a miserable donation, do you think the martyrs allowed themselves to be burnt alive so that you could walk into Paradise as if it were a windmill? As for the Saints, you won't save your souls by purchasing their merits, but in working to acquire their virtues!

A PEASANT: Then I'd rather hang myself and be damned outright. A man can't become a saint when he has to work sixteen hours a day.

TETZEL [*to the* PEASANT]: Hold your tongue, you fat fool! No one's asking you to be a saint. Buy a little indulgence from time to time, and God will make room for you through His infinite mercy.

GOETZ: Go ahead! Lay out your money on his trumpery

rubbish. He'll make you spend a ducat or two for the right to return to your miserable vices, but God won't ratify the transaction! You're rushing headlong down to Hell.

TETZEL: Take away their hope! Take away their faith! Their courage! What will you put in their place?

GOETZ: Love.

TETZEL: What do you know of love?

GOETZ: What do you know of love yourself? How could you love these men, you who despise them enough to try and sell them Paradise?

TETZEL [*to the* PEASANTS]: I, my lambs, do I despise you?

ALL: Oh!

TETZEL: I, my little chickens, do I not love you?

THE PEASANTS: Yes, yes! Of course you love us!

TETZEL: I am the Church, my brothers: and outside the Church, there is no love. Holy Church is our universal mother: through her monks and her priests, she dispenses the same maternal love to all her sons, to the most unfortunate, as to the most pampered favourites of life. [*A hand-bell rings, and a rattle sounds. The* LEPER *appears. The* PEASANTS *huddle away at the far end of the scene, terror-stricken.*] Who's this?

[*The* PARISH PRIEST *and the minor friars rush into the church.*]

THE PEASANTS [*pointing to the* LEPER]: There! There! Take care! The leper!

TETZEL [*horrified*]: Sweet Jesus!

[*A pause.* GOETZ *goes up to the* LEPER.]

GOETZ [*to* TETZEL, *pointing to the* LEPER]: Embrace him!

TETZEL: Pah!

GOETZ: If the Church loves without revulsion or recoil the most despicable of her sons, why do you hesitate to embrace him? [TETZEL *shakes his head.*] Jesus would have taken him in His arms. I love him better than you. [*Pause. He goes to the* LEPER.]

THE LEPER [*between his teeth*]: Here comes another to pull the trick of the leper's kiss.

GOETZ: Come here, my brother.

THE LEPER: I thought so! [*He goes to* GOETZ *unwillingly.*] If it's a question of your salvation, I cannot refuse, but do it quickly. You're all the same; you'd think the Lord had given me leprosy expressly to give you a chance to earn your place in Heaven. [*As* GOETZ *approaches him*] Not on the mouth! [GOETZ *kisses him on the mouth.*] Pah! [*He wipes his lips.*]

TETZEL [*beginning to laugh*]: Well? Are you satisfied? Look at him wiping his lips. Is he less of a leper now than he was before you kissed him? Tell me, leper, how goes the world with you?

THE LEPER: It would be better if there were fewer sound men and far more lepers.

TETZEL: Where do you live?

THE LEPER: With other lepers in the forest.

TETZEL: What do you do all day?

THE LEPER: Tell each other leper stories.

TETZEL: Why have you come down to the village?

THE LEPER: I came to see if I could pick up an indulgence.

TETZEL: Wonderful!

THE LEPER: Is it true that you can sell them?

TETZEL: For half a ducat.

THE LEPER: I haven't a penny.

TETZEL [*triumphantly, to the peasants*]: Watch this carefully! [*To the* LEPER] Do you see this shiny new indulgence? Which would you rather? That I should give it to you, or that I should kiss your lips?

THE LEPER: Well ...

TETZEL: Oh, I will do whichever you like. Choose.

THE LEPER: Well, I'd rather you gave me the paper.

TETZEL: Here it is, *gratis pro Deo* – it's a gift from your Holy Mother Church. Take it.

THE LEPER: Hurrah for the Church! [TETZEL *throws him the parchment. The* LEPER *catches it.*]

TETZEL: Now, go home quickly.

[*The* LEPER *goes. Sound of the bell, and the rattle.*]

TETZEL: Well? Which of us two loves him the better?

THE CROWD: You do! You do! Hurrah for Tetzel!

TETZEL: Come along, my brothers! Who's next? For your sister who died in a foreign land? [*Flute*] For your aunts who brought you up? For your mother? For your father and your mother – for your eldest son! Pay up! Pay! Pay!

GOETZ: Dogs! [*He strikes the table, sweeping the drum off the top, and it rolls away to the foot of the steps.*] Christ drove the money-changers out of the Temple ... [*He stops, looking at the silent and hostile peasants, pulls the hood down over his face and throws himself on his knees against the wall of the church, groaning.*] Ah! Ah! Ah! Shame on me! Shame on me! I don't know how to speak to them. Lord, I implore Thee, show me the way to their hearts!

[*The peasants watch him;* TETZEL *smiles: the peasants look at* TETZEL. TETZEL *winks, lays his finger on his lips to impose silence, and jerks his head in the direction of the church door. He tiptoes into the church. The peasants enter the church, carrying the plaster saint. They all disappear. A moment of silence, then* HEINRICH *appears in the doorway in lay clothes.*]

HEINRICH [*making his way towards* GOETZ]: You seem to think souls are like vegetables.

GOETZ: Who is that?

HEINRICH: The gardener can decide what is best for his carrots, but no one can direct the salvation of others.

GOETZ: Who is that speaking? Heinrich?

HEINRICH: Yes.

GOETZ [*rising and throwing back his hood*]: I was sure I should see you again after my first mistake. [*Pause*] What have you come to do? Nourish your hatred?

HEINRICH: 'Whoever sows Good shall reap only Good.' You said that, didn't you?

GOETZ: Yes, I did say it, and I will say it again. [*Pause*]

HEINRICH: I come to bring you the harvest.

GOETZ: It is too soon to reap. [*Pause*]

HEINRICH: Catherine is dying: there is your first crop.

GOETZ: She is dying? God receive her soul. What do you want me to do? [HEINRICH *laughs.*] Don't laugh, imbecile! You can see that you don't know how to laugh.

HEINRICH [*excusing himself*]: He's pulling faces at me.

GOETZ [*turning round swiftly*]: Who? [*He understands.*] Ah!

[*Turning back to* HEINRICH] I see – so now he is with you always.

HEINRICH: Yes, always.

GOETZ: He must be company for you.

HEINRICH [*passing his hand over his face*]: He makes me tired.

GOETZ [*going to* HEINRICH]: Heinrich ... If I have hurt you, forgive me.

HEINRICH: Forgive you? So that you can boast everywhere that you have changed hatred into love as Christ changed the water into wine.

GOETZ: Your hatred belongs to me. I will deliver you from your hatred and from the Devil.

HEINRICH [*in a changed voice, as if someone else were speaking through his mouth*]: In the name of the Father, the Son, and the Holy Ghost. I am the Father, the Devil is my son: hatred is the Holy Ghost. You could more easily divide the Holy Trinity than split our Trinity into three parts.

GOETZ: Then good night. Go back and say your masses in Worms. We shall meet again in nine months.

HEINRICH: I shall never go back to Worms, and I will never again say a mass. I no longer belong to the Church, jester. I have been forbidden to celebrate the offices and administer the holy sacraments.

GOETZ: What do they reproach you with?

HEINRICH: Taking money to betray the city.

GOETZ: It's a monstrous lie.

HEINRICH: I told the lie myself, I stood up in the pulpit and confessed everything before them all: my love of money, my jealousy, my disobedience, and my carnal desires.

GOETZ: You were lying!

HEINRICH: Why not? Everywhere in Worms they were saying that the Church abominated the poor, and the Church had ordered me to deliver the poor to the sword. We had to find a pretext for the Church to disown me.

GOETZ: You have expiated your sin.

HEINRICH: You know that no one ever expiates a sin.

GOETZ: You are right. Nothing can efface nothing. [*Pause.*

Suddenly he goes to HEINRICH.] What is happening to Catherine?

HEINRICH: Her body is covered with sores – her blood is rotting away. For three weeks she has neither eaten nor slept.

GOETZ: Why did you not stay with her?

HEINRICH: She is no concern of mine, nor I of hers.

[NASTI *enters and remains in the background.*]

GOETZ: She must be nursed,

HEINRICH: She cannot be cured. She will certainly die.

GOETZ: What is she dying of?

HEINRICH: Of shame. Her body revolts her because of all the men's hands that have been laid upon it. Her heart disgusts her even more because your image has remained within it. Her mortal sickness is you.

GOETZ: All that happened last year, priest, and I no longer recognize the sins of a year ago. I will pay for this sin in the next world and for all Eternity. But in this world, it is over. I have no time to waste.

HEINRICH: Then there are two men named Goetz.

GOETZ: Two, yes. A living Goetz who lives by Good, and a dead Goetz who lived by Evil.

HEINRICH: And you buried your sins with the dead Goetz?

GOETZ: Yes.

HEINRICH: Excellent. Only it isn't a dead man who is killing Catherine, but the fine, brave Goetz himself, the one who is devoting himself to living by love.

GOETZ: You're lying! It was the evil-doing Goetz who committed the crime.

HEINRICH: No crime has been committed. When you deflowered her you gave her far more than you possessed yourself: you gave her love. She really loved you, though I don't know why. And then, one fine day, divine grace touched you, so you pressed a purse in Catherine's hands, and drove her away. She is dying for your sake.

GOETZ: Could I have gone on living with a whore?

HEINRICH: Yes, because you made her what she is.

GOETZ: I had to renounce Good or give her up.

HEINRICH: If you had kept her, you might have saved her, and yourself with her. But save one soul – save only one? How could a man like Goetz stoop so low? He had much more important projects.

GOETZ [*abruptly*]: Where is she?

HEINRICH: On your own lands.

GOETZ: She wanted to see me again?

HEINRICH: Yes. And then Evil struck her down.

GOETZ: Where is she?

HEINRICH: I will not tell you: you have done her harm enough.

GOETZ [*raising his fist, furious*]: I ... [*He controls himself.*] Very well, I will find her again myself. Farewell, Heinrich. [*He bows in the direction of the Devil.*] My respects. [*He turns back towards* NASTI.] Nasti, come with me. [*He goes.*]

HEINRICH [*amazed*]: Nasti!

[NASTI *tries to follow* GOETZ. HEINRICH *stands in his way.*]

HEINRICH [*timidly*]: Nasti! [*More loudly*] Nasti, I was looking for you. Stop! I must talk to you. Despise me as much as you please, provided you listen to me. I have come from Schulheim. The revolt is preparing.

NASTI: Let me pass. I know that.

HEINRICH: Do you want this revolt to break out? Tell me, is that what you want?

NASTI: Is that any concern of yours? Let me pass.

HEINRICH [*stretching out his arms*]: You shall not pass without answering me.

[NASTI *looks at him in silence then makes up his mind.*]

NASTI: Whether I want it or not, no one can prevent it now.

HEINRICH: I can. In two days, I can build a dyke to contain this flood. In exchange, Nasti, I want you to forgive me.

NASTI: Still playing the game of forgiveness? [*Pause*] It is a game that bores me. I am not concerned with this. I have no right to condemn or absolve. Those matters concern only God.

HEINRICH: If God allowed me to choose between His pardon and yours, it is yours that I would choose.

NASTI: Then you would choose wrongly: you would renounce Paradise for a mere breath.

HEINRICH: No, Nasti: I should be renouncing the forgiveness of Heaven for the forgiveness of earth.

NASTI: Earth cannot forgive.

HEINRICH: You make me tired.

NASTI: What?

HEINRICH: I wasn't speaking to you. [*To* NASTI] You don't make my task easy: I am being driven into hatred, Nasti: I am being driven into hatred and you are refusing to help me. [*He crosses himself three times.*] There, I am quiet now for a moment, so listen to me. Quickly. The peasants are organizing themselves. They are going to negotiate with the barons. That will give us a few days.

NASTI: What will you do with them?

HEINRICH [*pointing to the church*]: You saw them; they will let themselves be torn in pieces for the Church: there is more piety in the countryside than in all the cities of Germany.

[NASTI *shakes his head.*]

NASTI: Your priests are powerless: the people love them, true, but if they condemn the rising, they will find themselves preaching in a desert.

HEINRICH: I'm not counting on their sermons, but on their silence. Imagine: one fine day, they wake up, the villagers find the door of their church open, and the church itself standing empty. The bird will have flown. No one before the altar, no one in the sacristy, no one in the crypt, no one in the presbytery ...

NASTI: Is this possible?

HEINRICH: All is prepared. Have you men?

NASTI: A few.

HEINRICH: Let them go through the land, shouting louder than anyone, blaspheming in particular. They must provoke scandal and horror. Then, at Righi, next Sunday, let them carry off the priest in the middle of the mass. Let them drag him into the forest and return with their swords stained with blood. All the priests of the region will leave their villages in secret the following night, and assemble at the castle of

Markstein, where they will be expected. On Monday morning, God returns to Heaven. Children will no longer be baptized, sins will no longer be absolved, and the sick will fear to die without confession. Fear will stifle the revolt.

NASTI [*reflecting*]: That might well be ... [*The door of the church opens. Snatches of organ music. The peasants come out, still carrying the saint. Looking at them*] If it might be, then it shall be ...

HEINRICH: Nasti, I implore you, if this enterprise succeeds, tell me you will forgive me.

NASTI: I will say it if you like. The trouble is that I know who you are.

CURTAIN

*

SCENE SIX

The interior of the church a fortnight later. All the villagers have taken refuge inside the church, and now no longer leave it. They eat and sleep there. At this moment, they are praying. NASTI *and* HEINRICH *are watching. Men and women are lying here and there on the pavement: the aged and infirm have also been carried into the church. Some are groaning and writhing at the very foot of the pulpit.*

NASTI [*to himself*]: I can't listen to them any more! Alas! You have nothing but your anger, and I have blown upon it to extinguish it.

HEINRICH: What are you saying?

NASTI: Nothing.

HEINRICH: You aren't content.

NASTI: No.

HEINRICH: Everywhere the people are crowding into the churches: they are held in a grip of fear, and the revolt has been strangled before it was born. What more can you want?

[NASTI *is silent.*] I shall rejoice for both of us. [NASTI *strikes him.*] What's come over you?

NASTI: If you dare rejoice, I'll break your neck.

HEINRICH: You don't want me to celebrate our victory?

NASTI: I won't allow you to rejoice because you have brought these people to their knees.

HEINRICH: What I have done, I did for you and with your full consent. Are you beginning to doubt your own powers, prophet? [NASTI *shrugs his shoulders.*] And yet this isn't the first time you have lied to them.

NASTI: It's the first time I've brought them to their knees and prevented them defending themselves; it's the first time I have made a weapon of superstition, and formed an alliance with the Devil.

HEINRICH: Are you afraid?

NASTI: The Devil is a creation of God; if God commands, the Devil will obey me. [*Brusquely*] I'm stifling in this church. Let us go.

[HEINRICH *and* NASTI *make a move to leave.* GOETZ *enters suddenly and strides up to* HEINRICH.]

GOETZ: Dog! You'll make use of any means to help you win your wager. You've made me waste a whole fortnight. I've searched my whole domain a dozen times to try and find her, and now I learn that she was here, while I was hunting for her miles away. Here, ill, dying on the stones. And by my fault. [HEINRICH *shakes himself free and goes out with* NASTI. GOETZ *repeats to himself*] By my fault ... No, nothing ... my voice is hollow. You want me to feel ashamed, and I have no shame. It is pride that sweats through all my wounds; for thirty-five years I have been rotting away with pride, and that is my way of dying of shame. We must change all that. [*Abruptly*] Destroy my power of thought! Destroy it! Make me forget myself! Transform me into an insect! So be it! [*The murmur of the peasants at their prayers swells and dies down.*] Catherine! [*He walks up and down among the crowd, looking at each face in turn and calling*] Catherine! Catherine! [*He goes back to a dark figure stretched on the paving, lifts the covering which hides it, and lets it fall back, reassured. Then he disappears behind a pillar, and we hear him calling again*] Catherine!

[*A clock strikes seven.*]

A SLEEPER [*lying on the stones, and waking with a start*]: What time is it? What day is it?

A MAN: Today is Sunday, and it is seven o'clock in the morning.

– No, it isn't Sunday.

– No more Sundays, no more Sundays. There'll never be another Sunday, our priest has taken them all away with him.

– He has left us the week-days, the cursed days of work and hunger.

THE PEASANT: Then everyone can go to the Devil. I'm going to sleep again. You can wake me for the Day of Judgement.

A WOMAN: Let us pray.

[HILDA *enters, carrying a truss of straw. She is followed by two peasant women, also carrying straw.*]

FIRST WOMAN: Hilda, it is Hilda!

SECOND WOMAN: We have missed you. What is happening in the world? Tell us. Tell us.

HILDA: There is nothing to tell. Silence everywhere, except for the animals who are crying because they are afraid.

A VOICE: Was the sun shining?

HILDA: I don't know.

A VOICE: Didn't you look at the sky?

HILDA: No. [*Pause*] I brought back some straw to make beds for the sick. [*To the two peasant women*] Help me. [*She helps a sick man rise and settle himself on a bed of straw.*] There. This one now. [*Same business*] And now this woman. [*They help lift an old woman who begins to sob.*] Don't cry, I implore you; don't take away their courage. Come along, grandma, if you begin to cry, they'll all start crying to keep you company.

THE OLD WOMAN [*snivelling*]: My rosary, there ... [*She points to the ground where she has been lying.*]

HILDA [*exasperated, picks up the rosary and throws it in her lap*]: Take it! [*She controls herself and says more gently*] Pray for us! Prayers are better than tears, they make less noise. Ah, no! You mustn't pray and cry at the same time. [*She wipes the old woman's eyes with her own handkerchief.*] There! There! Dry your eyes! It's all over! Don't cry any more; we are not guilty, and God has no right to have us punished.

THE OLD WOMAN [*still snivelling*]: Alas! my daughter! You know He has the right to do anything He pleases.

HILDA [*violently*]: If He has the right to punish the innocent, I will give myself directly to the Devil. [*They are all startled and look at her. She shrugs her shoulders and goes to lean against a pillar. She stands for a moment with fixed gaze, as if possessed by a memory, then suddenly, with disgust, she says*] Pah!

FIRST WOMAN: Hilda! What's the matter?

HILDA: Nothing.

FIRST WOMAN: You always know how to give us back our hope ...

HILDA: Hope in who? Hope in what?

THE WOMAN: Hilda, if you lose courage, we shall all lose courage too.

HILDA: Don't pay attention to anything I say. [*She shivers.*] It's cold. You are the only warmth left in the world. You must all cling together and wait.

A VOICE: Wait for what?

HILDA: To be warm again. We are hungry and thirsty, we are afraid, we are unhappy, but the only thing that matters is to keep warm.

THE WOMAN: Then come here against me. Come! [HILDA *does not move. The* WOMAN *rises and goes to her.*] Is she dead?

HILDA: Yes.

THE WOMAN: God receive her soul.

HILDA: God? [*A short laugh*] He will refuse it.

THE WOMAN: Hilda! How can you dare say that?

[*Murmurs among the crowd.*]

HILDA: She saw the flames of Hell before she died. Suddenly, she sat up, crying that she could see them, and then she died.

WOMAN: Is anyone with her?

HILDA: No one. Will you go and watch beside her?

THE WOMAN: Not for all the gold in the world.

HILDA: Very well. I'll go back there in a moment. Give me time to warm myself again.

THE WOMAN [*turning back towards the crowd*]: Let us pray, my brothers! Pray for pardon for a poor dead girl who has seen the flames of Hell and stands in danger of damnation.

HILDA [*in a low voice*]: Implore Thy pardon! What hast Thou to forgive us? It is Thou who shouldst ask our forgiveness! I have no thought of what You hold in store for me, and I did not even know that poor girl, but if You condemn her to damnation, I refuse to enter Heaven. Do You believe a thousand years of Paradise would make me forget the terror in her eyes? I have only scorn for Your elect – idiots, who have the heart to rejoice when there are damned souls writhing in hell and poor souls suffering on earth. I belong to the human race, and I will never desert my fellow beings; You have the power to let me die without confession, and summon me suddenly before Your bar of judgement; but we shall then see who will judge the other. [*Pause*] She loved him. All night long, she cried his name aloud. What sort of man is he, this bastard? [*She turns round abruptly towards the crowd.*] If you must pray, ask that the blood shed at Righi may be visited on the head of Goetz!

A VOICE: Goetz?

HILDA: He alone is guilty!

VOICES: May God punish Goetz the bastard!

[*During the preceding lines* GOETZ *has gradually drawn nearer.*]

GOETZ [*with a short laugh*]: There you have it! Whether I live by Evil or by Righteousness, I always find myself detested. [*To a peasant*] Who is that young woman?

THE PEASANT: That one? That is Hilda.

GOETZ: Hilda who?

THE PEASANT: Hilda Lemm. Her father is the richest miller in our village.

GOETZ [*bitterly*]: You listen to her as if she were an oracle. She tells you to pray for the damnation of Goetz, and you all throw yourselves on your knees.

THE PEASANT: Well, you see, we love her dearly.

GOETZ: You love her? She is rich and you still love her?

THE PEASANT: She isn't rich now. Last year, she was going to take the veil, and then during the famine, she gave up her vows to come and live among us.

GOETZ: What does she do to be beloved?

THE PEASANT: She lives like a holy sister, denying herself everything. She helps everyone ...

GOETZ: Yes, yes. I can do all that too. There must be something else, surely?

THE PEASANT: Nothing that I know.

GOETZ: Nothing? Indeed.

THE PEASANT: She ... she is lovable.

GOETZ [*beginning to laugh*]: Lovable? Thanks, my good man, you have enlightened me. [*He walks away.*] If she is really doing Good, I will rejoice. Lord, I will rejoice as is fit; provided Your kingdom is established, what matters whether it be through her means or through mine? [*He looks at* HILDA *with hostility.*] Like a holy sister! And I? Do I not live like a holy brother? What has she done that I cannot do also? [*He goes to her.*] Greetings! Do you know Catherine?

HILDA [*startled*]: Why ask me that? Who are you?

GOETZ: Answer me. Do you know her?

HILDA: Yes. Yes. I know her. [*She suddenly flings back the hood from his face and uncovers* GOETZ'S *face.*] And I know you too, although I have never seen you before. You are Goetz?

GOETZ: Yes, I am.

HILDA: At last!

GOETZ: Where is she?

[*She looks at him without replying, with an angry smile.*]

HILDA: You'll see her. There's no hurry.

GOETZ: Do you believe she wants to suffer five minutes longer?

HILDA: Do you believe her sufferings will cease when she sees you? [*She looks at him. Pause*] You will both have to wait.

GOETZ: Wait for what?

HILDA: Until I have had a good look at you, in my own time.

GOETZ: You're mad! I neither know you nor wish to know you.

HILDA: But I know you.

GOETZ: No.

HILDA: No? On your breast you have a tuft of curling hair, almost like a patch of velvet; to the left of your groin there is a purple vein, that swells and darkens when you're making love. Above your thigh there is a birthmark like a strawberry.

GOETZ: How do you know?

HILDA: For five days and nights I've been nursing Catherine. There were three of us in that room, she, you, and I. We shared our lives together for those five days. She saw you everywhere, and she made me see you too. Twenty times a night the door opened and you came into the room. You would stand there, looking at her, lazy and complacent, and then with two fingers, you would stroke her neck. Like this. [*She seizes his hand roughly.*] What power do they possess, these hands? What power? They are only flesh and hair ... [*She flings his hand violently from her.*]

GOETZ: What did she say?

HILDA: Everything needful to make me hold you in abhorrence.

GOETZ: That I was brutal, coarse, repellent?

HILDA: That you were handsome, brave, intelligent, that you were insolent, and cruel; that no woman could see you without desiring you.

GOETZ: She was talking of another Goetz.

HILDA: There is only one.

GOETZ: Then try to look at me with *her* eyes. Where's the cruelty? Where's the insolence? Alas, where is the intelligence? Before, I could see clear and far, because to do Evil is easy; but my sight has grown confused, and the world is filled with matters beyond my understanding. Hilda! I beg you! Please don't be my enemy.

HILDA: What can it matter to you, since I am without means to harm you?

GOETZ [*indicating the peasants*]: In their eyes, you have harmed me already.

HILDA: Those people belong to me and I to them: don't try and drag them into your problems.

GOETZ: Is it true they love you?

HILDA: Yes, it's true.

GOETZ: Why?

HILDA: I've never thought about it.

GOETZ: Bah! It's because you are beautiful.

HILDA: No, indeed, captain. You soldiers, you love fair women because you have nothing to do and you eat spiced dishes. My brothers here work all day long and they are hungry. They have no eyes for the beauty of women.

GOETZ: Then why is it? Because they need you?

HILDA: It is rather because I need them.

GOETZ: Why?

HILDA: You couldn't understand.

GOETZ [*going to her*]: Did they love you immediately?

HILDA: Immediately. Yes.

GOETZ [*to himself*]: That was just what I thought. Straight away or never. It's won or lost in advance: time and effort can do nothing for you. [*Abruptly*] God cannot desire that: it's unjust. You might as easily say some people are born damned.

HILDA: Some people have been. Catherine, for one.

GOETZ [*without listening*]: What did you do to them, sorceress? You must have done something to them to succeed; there where I failed?

HILDA: What did you do to infatuate Catherine? What did you do? [*They stare at each other, fascinated.*]

GOETZ [*still staring at her*]: You have robbed me of their love. When I look at you, it's their love that I see.

HILDA: When I look at you, it is Catherine's love that I see – and it fills me with horror.

GOETZ: What do you accuse me of?

HILDA: In Catherine's name, I accuse you of having driven her into despair.

GOETZ: That doesn't concern you.

HILDA: I reproach you, in the name of these men and women, of having flung your lands upon us in cartloads: and burying us underneath them.

GOETZ: Get out and be damned to you. I don't have to justify myself before a woman.

HILDA: I reproach you, in my own name, of having slept with me against my will.

GOETZ [*stupefied*]: Slept with you?

HILDA: For five nights running you possessed me by cunning or by force.

GOETZ [*laughing*]: It must have been in your dreams.

HILDA: In a dream, yes! It was a dream. Her dream, and she drew me into it. I wished to suffer with her suffering as I suffer with these others, but it proved a snare; for I had to love you with her love. God be praised! I see you. I see you in the light, and I have delivered myself. By daylight, you are no more than yourself.

GOETZ: Very well. Wake up from your dream. All this has happened in your head; I never touched you. Until today I had never seen you; nothing has ever happened to you.

HILDA: Nothing. Absolutely nothing. She cried out in my arms, what does it matter; nothing happened to me because you neither touched my breasts nor kissed my mouth. Yes, indeed, fine captain, you are as solitary as a rich man, and you've only suffered the wounds that have been dealt you – that is your misfortune. But I – I hardly feel my own body, I don't know where my life begins or where it finishes – I do not always answer when my name is called – so much does it astonish me, sometimes, that I have a name. But I suffer with all their bodies, I am struck on all their cheeks, I die with all their deaths. Every woman you have taken by force, you have violated in my flesh ...

GOETZ [*triumphantly*]: At last! [HILDA *looks at him, surprised.*] You will be the first.

HILDA: The first?

GOETZ: The first to love me.

HILDA: I? [*She laughs.*]

GOETZ: You love me already. For five nights I have held you in my arms – my mark is still upon you. In me you love the love that Catherine had for me, and in you I love the love these people bear you. You will love me. And if they're yours, as you pretend they are, then they must love me by your means.

HILDA: If I knew that one day my eyes would look on you with tenderness – I'd pluck them out immediately. [*He seizes her arm. She stops laughing and looks at him malignantly.*] Catherine is dead.

GOETZ: Dead! [*He is stunned by the news.*] When?

HILDA: A few moments ago.

GOETZ: Did she ... suffer?

HILDA: She saw the flames of Hell.

GOETZ [*staggering*]: Dead!

HILDA: She has escaped you, hasn't she? Why don't you go and stroke her neck!

[*Silence, then a disturbance at the back of the church. The peasants rise and turn towards the door. A moment of waiting. The noise increases, then* HEINRICH *and* NASTI *appear, carrying* CATHERINE *on a litter. She is no longer delirious, but she is half-sitting, and mutters to herself.*]

CATHERINE: No! No! No! No! No!

GOETZ [*in a cry*]: Catherine! [*To* HILDA] Carrion! You were lying!

HILDA: I ... I didn't lie to you, Goetz. Her heart had stopped beating. [*She bends over* CATHERINE.]

HEINRICH: We heard her crying from the street. She said the Devil was watching her. She implored us to carry her here to the foot of the cross.

[*The crowd begins to gather round them, menacing.*]

VOICES: No! No! She is damned! Away with her! Outside! Away with her at once!

GOETZ: By heaven, you dogs, I'll teach you Christian charity!

HILDA: Be quiet, you only know how to do harm. [*To the peasants*] She is only a body; the soul is clinging to the flesh because she is surrounded by devils. The Devil is lying in wait for you as well. Who will take pity on you if you will not take pity on her? Who will love the poor if the poor refuse to love among themselves? [*The crowd parts in silence.*] Carry her to the feet of Christ, since that is what she is asking.

[HEINRICH *and* NASTI *carry the litter to the foot of the cross.*]

CATHERINE: Is he there?

HILDA: Who?

CATHERINE: The priest.

HILDA: Not yet.

CATHERINE: Go and find him! Quick! I shall live until you bring him to me.

GOETZ [*approaching*]: Catherine!

CATHERINE: Is he here?

GOETZ: It is I, my love.

CATHERINE: You? Ah! I thought it was the holy priest. [*She begins to cry out.*] Find me the priest – please find him, quickly; I don't want to die without confession.

GOETZ: Catherine, you have nothing to fear – they will not do you any harm; you have suffered too much here on earth.

CATHERINE: I tell you I can see them.

GOETZ: Where?

CATHERINE: Everywhere. Asperge them with holy water. [*She begins to cry out again.*] Save me, Goetz – please save me: it was you who sinned – I cannot be guilty. If you love me, you must save me!

[HILDA *holds her in her arms and tries to make her lie down again.* CATHERINE *struggles, still crying out.*]

GOETZ [*imploringly*]: Heinrich!

HEINRICH: I am no longer of the Church.

GOETZ: She doesn't know it. If you will sign her forehead with the cross, you will save her from this final horror.

HEINRICH: To what end? She will find the horror on the farther side of death.

GOETZ: These are only visions, Heinrich!

HEINRICH: You think so? [*He laughs.*]

GOETZ: Nasti – you who say all men are priests ...

[NASTI *shrugs his shoulders and makes a helpless gesture of impotence.*]

CATHERINE [*without hearing them*]: Can't you see that I am dying? [HILDA *tries to make her lie down.*] Leave me alone! Leave me alone!

GOETZ [*to himself*]: If only I could ... [*Suddenly he makes a decision and turns to the crowd.*] It was through my sin that this woman is damned, and it is through my actions that she must now be saved. Leave us, all of you. [*The peasants go out slowly*, NASTI *dragging* HEINRICH. HILDA *hesitates.*] You too, Hilda. [*She gives him a long look and goes out.*] This time you're caught! However grudging You may be of miracles, this time You must work a miracle for me.

CATHERINE: Where are they going? Don't leave me alone.

GOETZ: No, Catherine, no, my love. I shall save you.

CATHERINE: What can you do? You aren't a priest.

GOETZ: I am going to ask Our Lord to give me all your sins. Do you understand?

CATHERINE: Yes.

GOETZ: I shall bear them all in your stead. Your soul will be as pure as on the day you were born. More pure than if the holy father had absolved you.

CATHERINE: How shall I know if God has answered your prayer?

GOETZ: I shall pray; if I return to you with my face ravaged by leprosy or gangrene, will you believe me?

CATHERINE: Yes, beloved. I will believe you.

[*He draws apart.*]

GOETZ: Lord – these sins of hers are mine – You know that. Render to me what rightfully belongs to me. You have no right to condemn this woman since I alone am guilty. Give me a sign! My arms are ready – my face and my breast are prepared. Blast my cheeks – let her sins become the poison oozing from my eyes and my ears; let them burn like an acid into my back, my thighs, and my sex. Strike me with leprosy, cholera, and the plague, but redeem and save her!

CATHERINE [*more feebly*]: Goetz! Goetz! Save me!

GOETZ: Can you hear me, God, or are You deaf? You cannot refuse this bargain, it is fair and just.

CATHERINE: Goetz! Goetz! Goetz!

GOETZ: Ah! I cannot endure that voice! [*He mounts the pulpit.*] Are You dead to mankind, yes or no? Look down on us: all mankind suffers. We must begin to die again. Mark me! Give me the wounds you bear! Give me the wound in Your right side, the two holes in Your hands. If a God could suffer for their sins, why not a man? Are You jealous of me?

Give me Your stigmata! Give me Your wounds! Give me Your wounds! [*He repeats this over and over like an incantation.*] Are You deaf! But of course! I'm being too stupid: God helps those who help themselves! [*He draws a dagger from his belt, stabs the palm of his left hand, then the palm of his right hand, and finally his side. Then he throws the knife behind the altar, and, leaning forward, marks the breast of the Christ with blood.*] Come back, all of you! [*The crowd returns.*] The Christ is bleeding. [*Murmurs. He raises his hands.*] See, in His infinite mercy, He has allowed me to suffer His stigmata. The blood of Christ, my brothers, the blood of Christ is flowing from my hands. [*He comes down the steps from the pulpit and goes to* CATHERINE.] My love, you need have no more fear. I touch your forehead, your eyes and lips with the blood of our dear Lord Jesus Christ. [*He marks her face with blood.*] Can you see them still?

CATHERINE: No.

GOETZ: Die in peace.

CATHERINE: Goetz – your blood – your blood. You have given your blood for my sake.

GOETZ: The blood of Christ, my Catherine ...

CATHERINE: Your blood ... [*She dies.*]

GOETZ: Kneel, all of you. [*They kneel.*] Your priests are curs: but you need have no fear. I shall remain with you; as long as the blood of Christ flows from these hands, no harm can ever touch you. Go back peacefully to your homes and rejoice – this is a holiday. Today, the kingdom of God begins for all men. We shall build the City of the Sun.

[*Pause. The crowd begins to disperse in silence. A woman passes close to* GOETZ, *seizes his hand and smears her face with blood.* HILDA *is the last to go. She comes to* GOETZ, *but he seems not to see her.*]

HILDA: Promise not to hurt them.

[GOETZ *does not reply. She goes.* GOETZ *staggers and leans against a pillar.*]

GOETZ: They are mine at last. At last.

CURTAIN

Act 3

SCENE SEVEN

A square at Altweiler.
Peasants are gathered around a peasant woman who is acting as their teacher. She is a young woman with a gentle air. She holds a stick, with which she is pointing to certain letters drawn out on the ground.

THE TEACHER: What is this letter?
A PEASANT: An L.
THE TEACHER: And this one?
ANOTHER PEASANT: An O.
THE TEACHER: And these two?
A PEASANT: N E.
THE TEACHER: No!
ANOTHER PEASANT: V E.
THE TEACHER: And the whole word?
A PEASANT: Love.
ALL THE PEASANTS: Love, Love ...
THE TEACHER: Courage, little brothers! Quite soon now you will all know how to read. You will be able to tell good from evil, and the true from the false. Now, tell me, you ... over there. ... What is our primary nature?
A PEASANT GIRL [*replying as if to a catechism*]: Our primary nature is the nature we all had before we knew Goetz.
THE TEACHER: What was that nature?
A PEASANT [*in the same tone*]: It was evil.
THE TEACHER: How must we combat our primary nature?
THE PEASANT: By creating a second nature.
THE TEACHER: How may we create a second nature?
A PEASANT GIRL: By teaching our bodies the gestures of love.
THE TEACHER: Are the gestures of love the same as love?
A PEASANT: No, the gestures of love are not ...

[HILDA *enters. The peasants stare at her.*]

THE TEACHER: What is it? [*She turns.*] Ah, Hilda! ... [*Pause*] My dear sister ... You make us uneasy.

HILDA: How can I do that? I am not saying anything.

THE TEACHER: You say nothing, but you are watching, and we know you don't approve of us.

HILDA: May I not think as I please?

THE TEACHER: No, Hilda. Here we all think aloud, in the clear light of day. The thoughts of each one belong to all. Will you not join us?

HILDA: No!

THE TEACHER: Then you do not love us?

HILDA: Yes, but in my own way.

THE TEACHER: Are you not happy to see our happiness?

HILDA: I ... Ah, my brothers, you have suffered so much; if you can be happy, then I must be happy too.

[*Enter* KARL *with a bandage over his eyes, led by a young woman.*]

THE TEACHER: Who are you?

THE YOUNG WOMAN: We are searching for the City of the Sun.

A PEASANT: You have arrived. This is the City of the Sun.

THE YOUNG WOMAN [*to* KARL]: I would have known it anywhere. What a pity you cannot see their happy faces; you would be happy too.

[*The peasants crowd round them.*]

THE PEASANTS: The poor things! Are you thirsty? Are you hungry? Come and sit down!

KARL [*sitting down*]: You are very kind.

A PEASANT: Everyone is kind here, because everyone is happy.

ANOTHER PEASANT: But in these troubled times, no one travels any more. We've only got each other to love. That's why your coming is such a joy.

A PEASANT WOMAN: It is sweet to be able to spoil a stranger. What can we do for you?

THE YOUNG WOMAN: We want to see the man with the bleeding hands.

KARL: Is it true that he can work miracles?

THE PEASANT WOMAN: He does nothing else.

KARL: Is it true that his hands bleed?

A PEASANT: Every day.

KARL: Then I would like him to put a little blood on my poor eyes, and give me back my sight.

A PEASANT WOMAN: Ah! Ah! He is just the man to do that. He will certainly cure you!

KARL: How fortunate you are, to possess such a man. None of you sin any more?

A PEASANT: No one drinks – no one steals.

ANOTHER PEASANT: Husbands are forbidden to beat their wives.

A PEASANT: Parents are forbidden to whip their children.

KARL [*sitting down on a bench*]: I hope it will last.

A PEASANT: It will last as long as it pleases God.

KARL: Alas! [*He sighs.*]

THE TEACHER: Why do you sigh?

KARL: This child has everywhere seen men in arms. The peasants and barons are going to fight.

THE TEACHER: Here, at Heidenstamm?

KARL: No, but all around.

THE TEACHER: In that case, we are not concerned. We don't wish harm to anyone, and our task is to establish the reign of love.

KARL: Bravo! Let them kill each other. Hatred, massacres, the blood of others are the necessary ingredients of your happiness.

A PEASANT: What do you mean? You're mad.

KARL: I only repeat what is being said everywhere.

THE TEACHER: What is being said?

KARL: That your happiness has made their sufferings more unbearable, and that despair has driven them to extremes. [*Pause*] Bah! You're quite right not to concern yourselves with others: a drop or two of blood sprinkled on your happiness, why not? It isn't too high a price to pay!

THE TEACHER: Our happiness is sacred. Goetz has said so. We are not happy for ourselves alone, but for everyone in the whole world. We witness to all and before all that happiness is possible. This village is a sanctuary, and all the peasants should turn their eyes towards us, as Christians turn towards the Holy Land.

KARL: When I return to my village, I will testify to this good news. I know whole families dying of hunger. They will be able to rejoice when they learn that you are happy for their sake as well. [*An embarrassed silence falls over the peasants.*] And tell me, good people, what will you do if this war does break out?

A PEASANT WOMAN: We shall pray.

KARL: Ah! I'm afraid you may be obliged to join the fight.

THE TEACHER: We refuse.

ALL THE PEASANTS: No! No! No!

KARL: Is not this a holy war, these slaves who are fighting for the right to become free men?

THE TEACHER: All wars are sacrilege. We shall remain as guardians of love and martyrs of the peace.

KARL: The barons will pillage, violate, kill your brothers at your gates, and you refuse to hate them?

A PEASANT WOMAN: We will pity them for being wicked.

ALL THE PEASANTS: We will pity them.

KARL: But if they are wicked, is it not just that their victims should rebel?

THE TEACHER: Violence is unjust from wherever it comes.

KARL: If you condemn the violence of your brothers, then you approve the conduct of the barons?

THE TEACHER: No, of course not.

KARL: But you must, since you have no desire that it should cease.

THE TEACHER: We desire that it should cease by the desire of the barons themselves.

KARL: And who will give them that desire?

THE TEACHER: We shall.

THE PEASANTS: We shall!

KARL: And until then, what should the peasants do?

THE TEACHER: Submit, wait, and pray.

KARL: Traitors, behold how you are unmasked; you have no love except for yourselves. But take care; if this war breaks out, you will be called upon to render an account and no one will tolerate that you should have remained neutral while your brothers were having their throats cut. If the peasants are victorious, beware lest they burn down the City of the Sun in order to punish you for having betrayed them. As for the lords, if they should win the battle, they will not allow a noble estate to remain in the hands of the serfs and peasants. To your arms, boys, to your arms. If you will not fight for fraternity, let it at least be in your own interest; happiness must be able to defend itself.

A PEASANT: We refuse to fight.

KARL: Then you will be defeated.

THE TEACHER: We will kiss the hand that strikes us, we shall die with prayers on our lips for those who kill us. As long as we live, we have always the possibility of letting ourselves be destroyed, but when we are dead, we will inhabit your souls, and our voices will echo in your ears.

KARL: God's blood, you know your lesson well. Ah! You are not guilty, the criminal is the false prophet who has filled your eyes with this mistaken sweetness.

THE PEASANTS: He insults our Goetz! [*They advance upon him.*]

THE YOUNG WOMAN: Will you strike a blind man, you who maintain that you live only for love?

A PEASANT [*snatching the bandage from* KARL'S *eyes*]: A fine sight indeed! See; it is Karl, the lackey from the castle. His heart is rotten with hate, and for weeks he has been prowling round, preaching discord and rebellion.

THE PEASANTS: Hang him! Hang him!

HILDA: My gentle sheep, are you grown so desperate? Karl is a cur, for he is driving you into war. But he speaks the truth, and I will not allow you to strike anyone who speaks true, whoever he may be. It is true, my brothers, that your City of the Sun is built on the misery of others; and for the barons to allow it, their peasants must resign themselves to slavery. My brothers, I do not reproach you for your happiness, but I felt much more at ease when we were all suffering together, for our misery was the misery of all men. On this earth that bleeds, all joy is obscene, and all happy men must live alone.

A PEASANT: You only love unhappiness – Goetz wants to build for the future!

HILDA: Your Goetz is an impostor. [*Murmurs*] Well? What are you waiting for? Why don't you beat me? Or hang me?

[GOETZ *enters.*]

GOETZ: What are these threatening looks?

A PEASANT: Goetz, he ...

GOETZ: Be quiet! I won't have these frowning brows. Smile first, you can tell me afterwards. Come along, smile.

[*The peasants smile.*]

A PEASANT [*smiling*]: This man has come to incite us to revolt.

GOETZ: So much the better – it will be a test. We must learn how to listen to words of hatred.

A PEASANT WOMAN [*smiling*]: He insulted you, Goetz, and called you a false prophet.

GOETZ: My good Karl, do you hate me so much?

KARL: Yes: as much as that.

GOETZ: Then it is because I didn't know how to make myself loved; forgive me. Escort him to the gates of the village, give them food, and the kiss of peace.

KARL: Everything will end in a massacre, Goetz. May the blood of these men be visited on your head.

GOETZ: So be it. [*They go out.*] Let us pray for their souls.

THE TEACHER: Goetz, there is one thing that torments us.

GOETZ: Speak.

THE TEACHER: It is to do with Hilda. We love her very much, but she makes us feel uneasy; she doesn't agree with you.

GOETZ: I know.

HILDA: What can it matter to you, since I am going away?

GOETZ [*surprised*]: You're going away?

HILDA: Very soon.

GOETZ: Why?

HILDA: Because these people are happy.

GOETZ: Well?

HILDA: I can be of no service to the content.

GOETZ: They love you.

HILDA: Of course, of course. But they'll get over it.

GOETZ: They still have need of you.

HILDA: Do you think so? [*She turns towards the peasants.*] Is it true that you still need me? [*Embarrassed silence from the peasants.*] You see. What service could I be to them, since they already have you? Farewell.

GOETZ [*to the peasants*]: Would you let her go without a word? Ingrates – who saved you from despair when you were desperate? Stay, Hilda – I am asking you, in their name. And you, I order you to give her back your love.

HILDA [*with sudden violence*]: Keep your love; you have stolen my purse, and you shall not give me back my own money as charity.

THE TEACHER: Stay, Hilda, since he desires it. We shall obey him. I swear it, and we shall all love you as the Holy Man commands.

HILDA: Sh! Sh! You all loved me with a natural impulse of your hearts: now it is over. Never speak of this again. Forget me, forget me quickly: the sooner you can forget me the better.

GOETZ [*to the peasants*]: Leave us.

[*All the peasants go out.*]

GOETZ: Where will you go?

HILDA: It doesn't matter. There's no lack of misery in the world.

GOETZ: Always misery! Always unhappiness! Is there nothing else?

HILDA: Nothing for me. That is my life.

GOETZ: Must you always suffer with their suffering? Can you not also rejoice with their happiness?

HILDA [*violently*]: No, I cannot! A fine happiness! They are bleating sheep. [*With despair*] Oh, Goetz, since you came among us, I am become the enemy of my own soul. When my soul speaks, I am ashamed of what it says to me. I know these people are no longer hungry, and they need not work so hard; if they desire this sheep-like happiness, I should desire it along with them. Well, I cannot, I cannot desire it. I must be a monster; I have less love for them since they have known less suffering. And yet, I cannot bear suffering. [*Pause*] Does it mean I am wicked?

GOETZ: You? No. You are jealous.

HILDA: Jealous. Yes. Enough to die of it. [*Pause*] You see, it's high time I went away; you have corrupted me. Wherever I go, whatever you undertake, you must sow hatred in men's hearts. Farewell.

GOETZ: Farewell. [*She does not move.*] Well? What are you waiting for? [*She makes a move to go.*] Hilda, I implore you, don't abandon me. [*She laughs.*] What is it?

HILDA [*without bitterness*]: You, you who have taken everything away from me, you now implore me not to abandon you?

GOETZ: The more they love me, the more I feel alone. I am their roof, and I have no roof. I am their heaven, and I have no heaven. Yes, I have one – it is this, and see how far away it is. I tried to make myself a pillar and carry the weight of the celestial vault. I'll tell you a secret; heaven is an empty hole. I even wonder where God lives. [*Pause*] I don't love these men enough; it all stems from that. I have made the gestures of love, but love did not follow; I suppose I am not very adroit. Why are you looking at me?

HILDA: You don't even love them. You have robbed me for nothing.

GOETZ: Ah! It wasn't their love I had to take from you, it was yours. I had to love them with your heart. Look, I envy you, down to your very jealousy. You stand there, you look at them, you touch them, you are warm, you are full of light, and you *are not myself*. It's intolerable. I cannot understand why we are still two people. I should like to become you, and still remain myself.

[NASTI *enters.*]

NASTI [*in a low voice*]: Goetz! Goetz! Goetz!

GOETZ [*turning round*]: Who is it? ... Nasti! ...

NASTI: All men are deaf.

GOETZ: Deaf? Deaf to your voice? This is new.

NASTI: Yes. It's new.

GOETZ: God puts you to the test like all the others? We'll see how you will acquit yourself.

NASTI: Let God test me as much as He pleases. I shall never

lose my faith in Him nor in my mission; and if He loses faith in me, then He is mad.

GOETZ: Speak.

NASTI [*pointing to* HILDA]: Send her away.

GOETZ: She is myself. Speak, or go away.

NASTI: Very well. [*Pause*] The revolt has begun.

GOETZ: What revolt? [*Brusquely*] It wasn't I! It wasn't my fault! Let them kill each other, I will have no part of it!

NASTI: They were only restrained by their fear of the Church: you proved they didn't need their priests; prophets are springing up everywhere. But they are prophets of anger, and they are preaching revenge.

GOETZ: And all that is my work?

NASTI: Yes, all.

GOETZ: Indeed! [*He strikes him.*]

NASTI: Strike! Strike again!

GOETZ: Ha! [*He swings away.*] How sweet Evil can be; I might have killed him! [*He walks up and down. Pause*] Well! What have you come to ask me?

NASTI: You can still prevent the worst.

GOETZ: I? [*A short laugh*] Idiot, I have the evil eye. How could you dare use my services?

NASTI: I have no choice. ... We have no arms, no money, no military leaders, and our peasants are too undisciplined to make good soldiers. In a few days, our reverses will begin; in a few months, the massacres.

GOETZ: So?

NASTI: There remains one hope. Today, I cannot control the revolt; in three months, I could direct it. If we can win one pitched battle, only one, the barons will sue for peace.

GOETZ: What is my part?

NASTI: You are the finest captain in Germany.

GOETZ [*gazes at him, then turns away*]: Ah! [*Pause*] Repair! I must always repair! You make me waste my time, all of you, whoever you are. Dear God, I have other things to do.

NASTI: You would let the whole world perish, provided you could build your City, your plaything, your model village?

GOETZ: This village is an arch. Love is sheltered beneath it; what matters the deluge, if I have saved love?

NASTI: Are you mad? You won't escape this war, it will come and seek you out in the midst of your precious shelter. [GOETZ *is silent.*] Well? Do you accept?

GOETZ: Not so fast. [*Pause. He returns to* NASTI.] There is no discipline; I shall have to create it. Do you know what that means? Hangings.

NASTI: I know.

GOETZ: Nasti, I shall have to hang these people. Hang them at random, to serve as examples; the innocent with the guilty. What am I saying? They are all innocent. Today, I am their brother, and I recognize their innocence. Tomorrow, if I become their leader, there will be none but the guilty, and I shall not understand any more; I shall hang.

NASTI: It must be done.

GOETZ: I shall have to turn myself into a butcher; you have neither weapons nor skill; force of numbers is your one card. I shall have to pour out lives. A horrible war!

NASTI: You will sacrifice twenty thousand to save a hundred thousand.

GOETZ: If only I could be sure! Nasti, you can believe me, I know what a battle is like; if we engage in this one, it's a hundred to one that we shall lose it.

NASTI: Then I take that single chance. Come! Whatever may be the designs of God, we are named as His elect; I am His prophet, and you are His butcher; there is no more time to draw aside.

[*Pause*]

GOETZ: Hilda!

HILDA: What is it?

GOETZ: Help me. What would you do in my place?

HILDA: I shall never be in your place, nor do I wish to be. You are the leaders of men, you others, and I am a mere woman. I have nothing to give you.

GOETZ: I have confidence only in you.

HILDA: In me?

GOETZ: Far more than in myself.

HILDA: Why should you want to make me an accomplice of your crimes? Why force me to decide in your place? Why give me power of life and death over my brothers?

GOETZ: Because I love you.

HILDA: Be quiet. [*Pause*] Ah! You have won; you have made me come over to the other side of the barricade; I was with those who suffered, now I am with those who decree the suffering. Oh, Goetz, I shall never sleep again. [*Pause*] I forbid you to shed blood. Refuse.

GOETZ: We will make the decision together?

HILDA: Yes. Together.

GOETZ: And we will endure the consequences together?

HILDA: Together whatever happens.

NASTI [*to* HILDA]: Why do you interfere?

HILDA: I speak in the name of the poor people.

NASTI: No one other than I has the right to speak in their name.

HILDA: Why?

NASTI: Because I am one of them.

HILDA: You, one of the people? You ceased to be that long ago. You are a leader.

[GOETZ *has been lost in thought, and has not heard them. He raises his head abruptly.*]

GOETZ: Why not tell them the truth?

NASTI: What truth?

GOETZ: That they don't know how to fight and they are lost if they begin this war.

NASTI: Because they will kill anyone who tells them so.

GOETZ: Supposing it was I who told them?

NASTI: You?

GOETZ: I have some credit with them because I am a prophet, and I gave them my possessions. What should one do with credit if not risk it?

NASTI: One chance in a thousand.

GOETZ: One chance in a thousand! Well! Have you the right to refuse?

NASTI: No. I have no right. Come.

HILDA: Don't go.

GOETZ [*taking her by the shoulders*]: Don't be afraid, this time God is on our side. [*He calls*] Come here, everyone. [*The peasants come back into the square.*] There is fighting everywhere. Tomorrow, all Germany will be in flames. I am going back among men to preserve our peace.

ALL THE PEASANTS: Alas, Goetz, do not abandon us. What shall we do without you?

GOETZ: I shall return, my brothers; here is my God, here is my happiness, here is my love; I shall return. Here is Hilda. I entrust you to her. If, during my absence, anyone should try to enlist you on one side or the other, refuse to fight. If you are threatened, reply to the threats with love. Remember, brothers, remember all of you; love can drive away this war. [*He goes out with* NASTI.]

THE PEASANTS: What if he doesn't come back? [*Silence*]

HILDA: Let us pray. [*A pause*] Pray that love may drive away this war.

THE PEASANTS [*kneeling*]: Oh Lord, let our love drive away this war.

HILDA [*standing in their midst*]: Oh Lord, let my love drive away this war. Amen.

[*The scene blacks out and the first lines of the eighth scene are picked up immediately following on* HILDA'S *prayer.*]

*

SCENES EIGHT AND NINE

The peasants' camp. Murmurs, and cries in the darkness.

VOICES: Hah! Hah! Hah!

GOETZ'S VOICE [*dominating the tumult*]: You will all die!

VOICES: Kill him! Kill him!

[*The lights come up on a clearing in the forest. It is night. Peasants armed with sticks and pitchforks. A few carry swords. Others hold torches.* GOETZ *and* NASTI *are standing on a rocky promontory, dominating the crowd.*]

VOICES: Hah! Hah! Hah!

GOETZ: My poor friends, you haven't even the courage to look the truth in the face?

A VOICE: The truth is that you are a traitor.

GOETZ: The truth, my brothers, the blinding truth, is that you haven't the least idea how to fight.

[*A peasant of herculean proportions strides forward.*]

THE HERCULES: I don't know how to fight? [*Laughter from the crowd*] Hey, friends, seems I don't know how to fight! Any time you like, I'll catch a bull by the horns and twist his ruddy neck off.

[GOETZ *jumps down from his rock, and comes to the man.*]

GOETZ: Well now, big brother, it seems you are three times as strong as I am?

THE HERCULES: I, little brother? [*He gives* GOETZ *a light tap which sends him staggering.*]

GOETZ: Exactly. [*To one of the peasants*] Give me that stick. [*To* THE HERCULES] And you, take hold of this one. On guard. Watch – pique, taille, sabre, estoque. [*He parries and dodges* THE HERCULES' *clumsy efforts to defend himself.*] You see! You see! You see! What good is your strength? You can only beat down the spirits of the air, and make the wind bleed. [*They fight.*] And now, my brother, forgive me. I'm going to knock you down a little. Only a very little. For the good of the assembly. There! [*He strikes the other down.*] Sweet Jesus, forgive me. [*The peasant falls.*] Are you convinced? He was the strongest among you, and I am far from being the most agile. [*Pause. The peasants are silent, amazed.* GOETZ *enjoys his victory for a moment, then takes up his argument again.*] Would you like me to tell you why none of you is afraid of death? Each one of you believes it will only strike his neighbour. [*Pause*] But now I am going to speak to God our Father, and ask Him a question. Father in Heaven, if it is Your desire I should help these poor creatures send me a sign to show which of them will perish in these wars. [*Suddenly he pretends to be afraid.*] Ho! Ho! Ho! Ho! What do I see? Ah, my brothers, what is happening to you! Oh, horrible vision! Ah, your fate is well and truly sealed!

A PEASANT [*worried*]: What's the matter with him? What's the matter? ...

GOETZ: God is melting your flesh like sealing-wax: I see nothing but your bones! Holy Virgin! All those skeletons!

A PEASANT: And what's that supposed to mean?

GOETZ: God has set His face against this revolt, and shows me in advance those who are marked for death.

THE PEASANT: Who do you mean?

GOETZ: Who? [*He points his finger at the peasant and thunders in a terrible voice*] You! [*Silence*] And you! And you! And you! What a macabre procession!

A PEASANT [*shaken, but still doubting*]: What proof have we that you are a real prophet?

GOETZ: Oh, men of little faith, if you must have your proof, behold this holy blood. [*He raises his hands. Silence. To* NASTI] I have won.

NASTI [*between his teeth*]: Not yet. [KARL *advances.*] Take heed of that one – he's the greatest menace.

KARL: Oh, too-credulous brothers, when will you learn to distrust your own eyes? Are you so tender and soft that you do not even know how to hate? Today, even today, a man merely has to speak in the name of the Lord to make you bow your heads. What has he done? There are a few drops of blood on his hands! A fine proof! If a man has to bleed before he can convince you, I can bleed too. [*He raises his hands, and they begin to bleed.*]

GOETZ: Who are you?

KARL: A prophet like yourself.

GOETZ: Prophet of wrath!

KARL: The only road which leads to true love.

GOETZ: I know you now. You are Karl, my lackey.

KARL: At your service.

GOETZ: A lackey-prophet – it's ridiculous.

KARL: Not more ridiculous than a general-prophet.

GOETZ [*coming down the steps*]: Show me your hands! [*He turns them over.*] Good heavens, this man has bladders filled with blood concealed in his sleeves.

KARL: Let me see your hands. [*He examines them.*] This man

scratches old wounds with his nails to squeeze out a few drops of pus. Come along, brothers, put us to the test, and decide which of us two is the true prophet.

MURMURS: Yes. ... Yes. ...

KARL: Can you do this? [*He makes a stick burst into flowers.*] Or this? [*He brings a rabbit out of his hat.*] And this? [*He is surrounded by a cloud of smoke.*] Show me anything you can do.

GOETZ: Conjuring tricks I have seen a hundred times in village fairs. I am no juggler.

A PEASANT: A prophet ought to be able to do anything a juggler does.

GOETZ: I shall not engage in a competition of miracles with my own body servant. My brothers, I was a general before I became a prophet. We are talking of war; if you will not believe the prophet, at least trust the general.

KARL: You will be able to trust the general when the general has proved that he is no traitor.

GOETZ: Ingrate! It was for love of you and your brothers that I despoiled myself of my belongings.

KARL: For the love of me?

GOETZ: Yes, for you who now hate me.

KARL: You mean, you love me?

GOETZ: Yes, my brother, I love you.

KARL [*triumphantly*]: He has betrayed himself, my brothers! He's lying to us all! Look at my mug and tell me how anyone can love me. And you, my friends, each and everyone of you, do you believe you are so lovable?

GOETZ: Idiots! If I did not love them, why should I have given them my lands?

KARL: Exactly. Why? There's the whole question. [*Brusquely*] God! God who sounds our hearts and our guts, help me now! I will lend You my body and my voice; tell us why Goetz the bastard gave away his lands. [KARL *begins to utter terrible cries.*]

THE PEASANTS: God is here! God will speak! [*They fall on their knees.*]

GOETZ: God! That's the last straw!

KARL [*he has closed his eyes and speaks in a strange voice which does not seem to be his own*]: Hola! Ho! Ho! The earth!

THE PEASANTS: Hola, ho! Hola, ho!

KARL [*as before*]: I, God, behold you; men of earth. I behold you.

THE PEASANTS: Have mercy upon us.

KARL [*as before*]: Is the man Goetz among you?

A PEASANT: Yes, Our Father, to the right, a little behind you.

KARL [*as before*]: Goetz! Goetz! Why did you give them your lands? Answer me.

GOETZ: To whom have I the honour of speaking?

KARL [*as before*]: I am the one who is.

GOETZ: Well, if you are who you are, then you know what you know, and you must know why I have done what I have done.

THE PEASANTS [*threateningly*]: Ah! Ah! Answer! Answer!

GOETZ: I will answer you, my brothers. You, not him. I gave away my lands so that all men might become equal.

[KARL *laughs.*]

THE PEASANTS: God is laughing! God is laughing!

[NASTI *has come down the steps and taken up a position behind* GOETZ.]

KARL [*as before*]: You lie, Goetz, you are lying to your true God.

And you, my sons, hear me!
Whatever a lord may do, he will never become your equal.
That is why I demand you should kill them all.
This one has given you his lands,
But are you able to give him yours?
He has the choice of bestowing or keeping,
But had you the chance to refuse?
To him who gives you blow or kiss
I command you to render kiss or blow;
But to him who gives what you are unable to render
Offer the hatred that is within your hearts.
For you are enslaved and he has enslaved you;
You are humiliated and he increases your humiliation:
Gift of the morning, grief!

Gift of the noontide, care!
Gift of the evening, despair!

GOETZ: A fine sermon! Who gave you life and light? It was the Lord God! The gift is His law, and whatsoever He does, He bestows upon you. What can you render Him, you who are nothing but dust? Nothing! Conclusion: it is God who deserves your hate.

THE PEASANTS: With God, it's different.

GOETZ: Why has He created us in His image? If God is generosity and love, man, His creatures, should be love and generosity! My brothers, I implore you; accept my gifts and my friendship. I do not ask you for gratitude, no indeed; I ask only that you should not condemn my love as a vice, and you should not reproach me for my gifts as if they were crimes.

A PEASANT: Talk away; me, I don't like charity.

KARL [*resuming his natural voice, and pointing to the beggar*]: Here's one who has understood. The lands are yours; whoever pretends to give them to you, is deceiving you, for he is giving away what is not his to give. Take his lands. Take and kill, if you wish to become men. For we can only teach ourselves by violence.

GOETZ: Is there to be nothing but hate, my brothers? My love for you ...

KARL: Your love is of the Devil, it destroys whatever it touches. Ah, my friends, if you could see the people of Altweiler; it only took him three months to turn them into geldings. He'll love you so well, he'll cut off all the cobblers in the country and pin them back with rosebuds. Don't let yourselves be deceived; you are animals, and hatred has changed you into men; if your hate is taken from you, you will fall back on all fours and into the voiceless misery of beasts.

GOETZ: Nasti! Help me!

NASTI [*pointing to* KARL]: The case is judged. God is with that man.

GOETZ [*stupefied*]: Nasti!

THE PEASANTS: Away with him! Away with him to the Devil!

GOETZ [*suddenly enraged*]: Yes, I'm going, don't be afraid. Run towards your death; if you get yourselves done in, I'll dance for joy. How hideous you are! Lemur-people! Larvae! I thank God for showing me your souls; for I know now that I was mistaken; it is right that the lords possess the land, for their souls are proud; it is right that you crawl on all fours, rooting, for you are nothing but pigs and swine!

THE PEASANTS [*preparing to throw themselves upon him*]: Kill! Kill!

GOETZ [*snatching a sword from a peasant*]: Come and take me!

KARL [*raising his hands*]: Enough. [*Silence*] This man trusted himself to your word. You must learn to keep it, even when it is given to an enemy.

[*The stage empties little by little, and the shadows fall once more. The last torch is fastened to the rock.* NASTI *takes it, and turns to go.*]

NASTI: Leave this place, Goetz; leave it quickly!

GOETZ: Nasti! Nasti! Why have you forsaken me?

NASTI: Because you failed.

GOETZ: Nasti, they are a pack of wolves. How can you remain among such people?

NASTI: All the love in the world is with them.

GOETZ: With them? If you found a grain of love among these dunghills you must have good eyesight. I didn't see anything.

NASTI: That's true, Goetz; you couldn't see anything. [*He goes.*]

[*It is night. The murmurs die away in the distance. Far away a woman cries out, then a faint light grows on* GOETZ.]

GOETZ [*alone*]: You will all die, dogs! I shall be mortal to you in memorable fashion. Come to me, my wickedness; pour into me, and render me light. [*Pause*] How strange. Good has purged my soul; there remains no drop of venom. Very well. Let me take the road for Good, let me take the road to Altweiler; they must hang me, or let me go on doing Good. My children are waiting, my chickens, my geldings, my angels of the farmyard; they will rejoice to see me. Oh God, how they all bore me. It is the others I love – the wolves. [*He begins to walk up and down.*] Very well, Lord, you must guide me through the dark night. Since we must persevere despite the failure, let all failure be to me a sign, all misery good luck, every accident a grace; give me the good use of my misfortunes. Lord, I believe, I must believe, that You permitted me to wind up outside the world because You desire to keep me for Yourself. Here I am, my God; here we are face to face again, like in the good old days when I was doing evil. Ah! I should never have interfered with men; they are a clog. They are the brushwood a man must part in order to come to You. I am coming, Lord, I come. I am walking in Your night; stretch out Your hand to help me. Tell me; You are indeed the night. Night, the tormenting absence of all! For You are He who is present in the universal absence, He whom we hear only when all is silence, He whom we see when we can see no more. Ancient night, huge night of before creation, night of non-knowing, night of disgrace and disaster, cover me, devour my foul body, slip between my soul and myself and destroy me. I demand the catastrophe, the shame and the loneliness of scorn, for man is made to destroy man in himself, and to open himself like a female to the huge dark body of the night. Until I can taste everything, I shall no longer desire anything, until I possess all, I shall possess nothing. I shall abase myself before all, and Thou, oh Lord, Thou wilt take me in the nets of Thy night, and raise me up above all men. [*He cries aloud in his agony.*] This hatred of men, this disdain of myself, did I not seek for them when I was still evil? The loneliness of Good, how am I to know it from the loneliness of Evil? [*The dawn begins to break slowly.*] The dawn is breaking. I have come through Your night. Blessed be Thou for Thy gift of light; I shall at last be able to see clearly. [*He turns and sees Altweiler in ruins.* HILDA *is sitting on a pile of stones and rubble, her head in her hands. He cries out:*]

GOETZ: Ah!

HILDA [*raising her head and looking at him*]: At last!

GOETZ: Where are the others? Dead? Why? Because they refused to fight?

HILDA: Yes.

GOETZ: Ah, give me back my night; hide me from the sight of men. [*Pause*] How did it happen?

HILDA: Peasants came from Walsheim with weapons in their hands; they asked us to join them, and we refused.

GOETZ: Then they set fire to the village. How easy. [*He bursts out laughing.*] Why didn't you die with the others?

HILDA: Are you sorry?

GOETZ: No survivors – so very much more simple.

HILDA: I am sorry, too. [*Pause*] They shut us in a house, and then set it on fire. It was a good idea.

GOETZ: Yes, a good idea, a very good idea.

HILDA: At the last minute, a window was forced open. I jumped out. I wasn't afraid to die, but I wanted to see you again.

GOETZ: What for? You would have seen me again in heaven.

HILDA: We shall not go to heaven, Goetz, and even if we do go, both of us, we shall have no eyes to see each other, no hands to touch each other. In heaven, you have no time for anything but God. [*She comes to touch him.*] Here you are; a little worn-out flesh, wrinkled, miserable; a life – a wretched life. It is this flesh and this life I love. You can only love on earth, and against the will of God.

GOETZ: I love only God, and I am no longer on this earth.

HILDA: Then you don't love me?

GOETZ: No. And neither do you, Hilda, you don't love me either. What you believe to be love is hatred.

HILDA: Why should I hate you?

GOETZ: Because you believe that I have killed your people.

HILDA: It was I who killed them.

GOETZ: You?

HILDA: It was I who said no. I loved them better dead than alive as murderers. Oh, God, what right had I to choose for them?

GOETZ: Bah! Do as I do! Wash your hands of all this blood. We are nothing; we have no power over anything. Man dreams he can act, but it is God who directs his actions.

HILDA: No, Goetz, no. But for me, they would still be alive.

GOETZ: Very well. So be it. But for you, perhaps. I am not concerned in this.

HILDA: 'We decided together, and we shall take the consequences together.' Remember?

GOETZ: We are not together. You wanted to see me? Well, look at me, touch me. Good. Now, go away. For the rest of my days, I shall see no more human beings. I shall have eyes for nothing but the earth and the stones. [*Pause*] I asked you a question, Lord, and You replied to me. Blessed be Thou who hast revealed the wickedness of men. I shall chastise their sins through my own flesh, I shall torment this body with hunger, cold, and the scourge; but slowly, very slowly. I shall destroy the man, because Thou hast created man for destruction. They were my people; only a few – a single village, almost a single family. My subjects lie dead, and I, the living, I am dead to the world. I shall spend the rest of my days meditating on dissolution. [*To* HILDA] Are you still there? Leave me. Go elsewhere to seek your life and your misery.

HILDA: The most miserable of all is before me. This is my place. I shall stay here.

CURTAIN

*

SCENE TEN

The ruined village, six months later.

Sitting in the same position as at the end of the previous scene, HILDA *is gazing towards the road. Suddenly, we realize she can see somebody coming. She half-rises, and waits.*

HEINRICH *enters, flowers stuck in his hat, a bouquet in his hand.*

HEINRICH: We've arrived. [*He turns to an invisible companion.*] Take off your hat. [*To* HILDA] My name is Heinrich; in the old days I used to say mass. Today I live on charity. [*To* THE DEVIL] Where are you off to? Come here. [*To* HILDA] When the smell of death is around, he has to be about his business. But he wouldn't really harm a fly.

HILDA: It's a year and a day, isn't it? A year and a day since Worms?

HEINRICH: Who told you?

HILDA: I counted the days.

HEINRICH: They've talked to you about me?

HILDA: Yes. A long time ago.

HEINRICH: A beautiful day, isn't it? I picked these flowers on the way; it's an anniversary bouquet. [*He holds them out to her.*]

HILDA: I don't want them. [*She lays them down beside her.*]

HEINRICH: You shouldn't be afraid of happy people.

HILDA: You aren't happy.

HEINRICH: I told you, this is a holiday; last night I even slept. Come along, little sister, give me a smile; I love all men except one, and I want everyone in the world to be happy. [*Brusquely*] Go and find him. [*She does not move.*] Go along! You mustn't keep him waiting.

HILDA: He isn't waiting for you.

HEINRICH: Isn't he? You surprise me. We are a couple of friends, and I'll take a bet he's made himself smart for this occasion.

HILDA: Spare him. Pick up your flowers and go away.

HEINRICH [*to* THE DEVIL]: D'you hear?

HILDA: Leave your Devil alone. I don't believe in him.

HEINRICH: Neither do I.

HILDA: Well, then?

HEINRICH [*laughing*]: Ha! ha! ha! You are a child.

HILDA: The man who harmed you is no more; he is dead to the world. He won't even know you again, and I am sure you could never recognize him. You are looking for one man, and in him you will find another.

HEINRICH: I will take what I find.

HILDA: Spare him, I implore you. Why should you want to hurt me? I have done you no harm?

HEINRICH: I wasn't meaning to hurt you; I like you very much.

HILDA: I shall bleed through all the wounds you deal him.

HEINRICH: You love him?

HILDA: Yes.

HEINRICH: Then it is possible to love him? How strange. [*He laughs.*] Many people have tried to love me. But without success. Does he love you?

HILDA: He has loved me as much as he loved himself.

HEINRICH: If he loves you, I won't be sorry to make you suffer.

HILDA: Forgive him his trespasses, and God will forgive you your own.

HEINRICH: But I don't want Him to forgive me in the least. Damnation has its good sides – the whole answer is to adapt yourself. And I have done that. I am not yet in Hell, and already I have my little habits.

HILDA: Poor man.

HEINRICH [*angry*]: No! No! No! I am not a poor man. I am happy, I tell you I am happy. [*Pause*] Come along! Call him. [*She is silent.*] It would be better for you to call him; and then he'll have a surprise when he sees me here. Won't you call him? I'll call him myself. Goetz! Goetz! Goetz!

HILDA: He isn't here.

HEINRICH: Where is he?

HILDA: In the forest. Sometimes he stays there for weeks on end.

HEINRICH: Far from here?

HILDA: Twenty-five leagues.

HEINRICH [*to* THE DEVIL]: Do you believe her? [*He closes his eyes and listens to the whisperings of* THE DEVIL.] Yes. Yes. Yes. [*He smiles maliciously.*] Well, how am I to find him?

HILDA: Go and look, good father. Go and look. Your companion will know how to guide you.

HEINRICH: God keep you, my sister. [*To* THE DEVIL] Come along. This way.

[*He disappears.* HILDA *is left alone, and watches him out of sight.* GOETZ *enters, carrying a whip in his right hand, a pitcher in his left. He seems exhausted.*]

GOETZ: Who was calling me? [HILDA *does not reply.*] Someone was here and called me. I heard his voice.

HILDA: You always hear voices when you are fasting.

GOETZ: Where did those flowers come from?

HILDA: I picked them myself.

GOETZ: You don't often pick flowers. [*Pause*] What is today? What day of the year?

HILDA: Why ask me that?

GOETZ: Someone was to come in the autumn.

HILDA: Who?

GOETZ: I don't know any more. [*Pause*] Tell me. What is today? What day of what month?

HILDA: Do you think I count the days? We have only one now, that begins and begins again; it is given to us with the dawn, and taken away with the night. You are a clock that has run down, and tells always the same time.

GOETZ: Run down? No; I have gained. [*He shakes the pitcher.*] Can you hear? It gurgles. The water makes a heavenly music; I have Hell in my throat and Paradise in my ears.

HILDA: How long is it since you drank?

GOETZ: Three days. I have to hold out till tomorrow.

HILDA: Why until tomorrow?

GOETZ [*laughing like an idiot*]: Ha! Ha! I must! I must! [*Pause. He shakes the pitcher.*] Glug! Glug! Hey? I don't know any sound more unpleasant for a man dying of thirst.

HILDA: Amuse yourself, torment your desires. Drink when you're thirsty – that would be very much too simple! If you didn't harbour a temptation eternally in your soul, you'd run the risk of forgetting yourself.

GOETZ: How am I to conquer myself, if I don't give myself temptations?

HILDA: Oh, Goetz, do you really believe you are living this day for the first time? The pitcher, the sound of the water, the blanched skin of your lips, I know all that by heart. Don't you know what is going to happen?

GOETZ: I shall hold out till tomorrow; that is all.

HILDA: You have never held out to the end because you set yourself impossible tests. You are going to shake that pitcher until you collapse. When you have fallen, I will have to make you drink.

GOETZ: You want something new? Look. [*He tilts the pitcher.*] The flowers are thirsty. Drink, little flowers, drink up this water, let my Heaven visit your gullets of gold. Look. They are reviving. The earth and the flowers accept my gifts; it is only men who reject them. [*He overturns the pitcher.*] And now see; no way of drinking now. [*He laughs and repeats painfully*] No way ... no way ...

HILDA: Is it God's will that you should become childish?

GOETZ: Of course. Man has to be destroyed, hasn't he? [*He throws away the pitcher.*] See if you can make me drink now! [*He falls.*]

HILDA [*looks at him coldly, then begins to laugh*]: You know quite well I always have water in reserve; I know you. [*She fetches a jug of water, then returns and lifts up his head.*] Come along, drink.

GOETZ: Not before tomorrow.

HILDA: God wishes you to be childish or a fool, but not dead. Therefore, you must drink.

GOETZ: I make all Germany tremble, and yet here I lie on my back like a suckling babe in the hands of his nurse. Are You satisfied, Lord? Do You know any abjection worse than my own? Hilda, you who foresee everything, if I quench my thirst, do you know what will happen afterwards?

HILDA: Yes, I know. The great game, the temptation of the flesh; you will want to go to bed with me.

GOETZ: And even so you want me to drink?

HILDA: Yes.

GOETZ: Supposing I were to try and rape you?

HILDA: In the state you're in? Don't be foolish; everything is as carefully planned as in the mass. You will shout obscenities and insults, and then to finish up you will whip yourself. Drink.

GOETZ [*taking the jug*]: Another defeat! [*He drinks.*] A man's body is disgusting. [*He drinks.*]

HILDA: Your body is sound. The rottenness is in your soul.

GOETZ [*setting down the jug*]: My thirst has gone; I feel empty. [*Pause*] I am tired.

HILDA: Sleep.

GOETZ: No, because I am tired. [*He looks at her.*] Show me your breasts. [*She does not move.*] Go on, show them, tempt me; make me burst with desire. No? Ah! bitch, why not?

HILDA: Because I love you.

GOETZ: Heat your love till it is white hot, plunge it into my heart, let it sizzle and smoke! If you love me, you must torture me.

HILDA: I belong to you; why should I make my body a rack for your torment?

GOETZ: If you could see into my mind, you would smash my face. My mind is a witches' sabbath, and you are all the witches.

HILDA [*laughing*]: You are boasting.

GOETZ: I wish you were a beast so that I could mount you like an animal.

HILDA: How you suffer because you are a man.

GOETZ: I am not a man, I am nothing. There is nothing but God. Man is an optical illusion. I disgust you, don't I?

HILDA [*calmly*]: No, because I love you.

GOETZ: You can see I am trying to degrade you.

HILDA: Yes, because I am your most precious possession.

GOETZ [*angrily*]: You are not playing the game!

HILDA: No, I am not playing the game.

GOETZ: As long as you remain beside me, I shall not feel altogether unclean.

HILDA: That is why I remain.

[GOETZ *rises painfully.*]

GOETZ: If I took you in my arms, would you shrink from me?

HILDA: No.

GOETZ: Even if I come to you with my heart filled with horrors?

HILDA: If you can bring yourself to touch me, it is because your heart is pure.

GOETZ: Hilda, how can we love each other without shame? The sin of lust is the most degrading of vices.

HILDA: Look at me, look at me well, look at my eyes, my lips, my breasts, and my arms; am I a sin?

GOETZ: You are beautiful. Beauty is Evil.

HILDA: Are you sure?

GOETZ: I am sure of nothing. [*Pause*] If I gratify my desires, I sin, but I free myself of desires; if I refuse to satisfy them, they infect the whole soul. ... Night is falling; at twilight a man needs good eyesight to distinguish the good Lord from the Devil. [*He approaches her, touches her, then springs away.*] Sleep with you under the eye of God? No; I don't care for drunken couplings. [*Pause*] If I could know a night deep enough to hide us from His regard.

HILDA: Love is that deep night; when people love each other, they become invisible to God.

[GOETZ *hesitates, then springs away from her.*]

GOETZ: Give me the eyes of the Boeotian lynx so that my gaze may penetrate this skin. Show me what is hidden in your nostrils and inside your ear-holes. I who would shudder to touch dung with my finger-tips, how can I desire to hold in my arms the sack of excrement itself?

HILDA [*violently*]: There is more filth in your soul than within my whole body. The ugliness and filth of the flesh is in your soul alone. I have no need of the eyes of a lynx; I have nursed you, washed you, known the odours of your fever. Have I ever ceased to love you? Each day you grow a little more like the corpse you will become, and I still love you with all my heart. If you die, I will lie down beside you, and stay there to the very end, without eating or drinking; you will rot away in my embrace, and I will love your carrion flesh; for you do not love at all, if you do not love the all.

GOETZ [*holding out the whip*]: Whip me. [HILDA *shrugs her shoulders.*] Come along, beat me, beat me, take vengeance upon me for Catherine dead, your youth lost, and all those people burnt alive by my fault.

HILDA [*bursting out laughing*]: Yes, I will beat you, filthy monk;

I will beat you because you have ruined our love. [*She takes the whip.*]

GOETZ: Across the eyes, Hilda, across the eyes!

HEINRICH [*entering*]: Whip away! Whip away! Carry on exactly as if I were not here. [*He comes forward. To* HILDA] My friend here whispered to me to take a little walk, and then come back very softly. You can't deceive that one, you know. [*To* GOETZ] She wanted to prevent our meeting. Is it true you weren't expecting me?

GOETZ: I? I was counting the days.

HILDA: You counted them? Oh! Goetz, you lied to me. [*She looks at him.*] What's the matter? Your eyes are shining, you are no longer the same.

GOETZ: It is the joy of seeing him again.

HILDA: A strange joy; he'll do you all the harm he can.

GOETZ: It is proof that he loves me. You are jealous, eh? [*She doesn't reply. He turns back to* HEINRICH.] Was it you picked the flowers?

HEINRICH: Yes. For you.

GOETZ: Thank you. [*He picks up the bouquet.*]

HEINRICH: Happy anniversary, Goetz.

GOETZ: Happy anniversary, Heinrich.

HEINRICH: Tonight, you are probably going to die ...

GOETZ: Indeed? Why?

HEINRICH: The peasants are looking for you to kill you. I had to come quickly to get here before them.

GOETZ: Kill me, by Christ! That's honouring me beyond my deserts; I thought I had been completely forgotten. And why do they want to kill me?

HEINRICH: Last Thursday, on the plain of Gunsbach, the barons cut Nasti's army to ribbons. Twenty-five thousand dead; it was a complete rout. In two or three months the revolt will be stamped out.

GOETZ [*violently*]: Twenty-five thousand dead! They should never have engaged in that battle! The idiots! They should have ... [*He controls himself.*] The devil. We are all born to die. [*Pause*] They lay it all to my door, naturally?

HEINRICH: They say you would have avoided the butchery if

you had accepted the leadership of the troops. You can be happy. You are the best-hated man in all Germany.

GOETZ: And Nasti? Is he in flight? A prisoner? Dead?

HEINRICH: Guess.

GOETZ: Go to hell. [*He becomes lost in thought.*]

HILDA: Do they know he is here?

HEINRICH: Yes.

HILDA: Who told them? You?

HEINRICH [*pointing to* THE DEVIL]: Not me. Him.

HILDA [*gently*]: Goetz! [*She touches his arm.*] Goetz!

GOETZ [*startled*]: Ha! What is it?

HILDA: You cannot stay here.

GOETZ: Why not? I must pay, mustn't I?

HILDA: You have nothing to pay for – you are not guilty.

GOETZ: Mind your own business.

HILDA: This is my business. Goetz, you must go.

GOETZ: Go where?

HILDA: No matter where, provided you are safe. You have no right to get yourself killed.

GOETZ: No.

HILDA: It would be cheating.

GOETZ: Ah yes; cheating. Well? Haven't I cheated all my life? [*To* HEINRICH] Begin your interrogation; this is the moment, I am ready.

HEINRICH [*meaning* HILDA]: Tell her to go away.

HILDA: You will have to talk in front of me. ... I am not going to leave him.

GOETZ: He is right, Hilda; this trial must be judged in private.

HILDA: What trial?

GOETZ: Mine.

HILDA: Why let him put you on trial? Drive away this priest and let us leave the village.

GOETZ: Hilda, I need to be put on trial. Every day, every hour, I condemn myself, but I can never convince myself because I know myself too well to trust myself. I cannot see my soul any longer, because it is under my nose; I need someone to lend me his eyes.

HILDA: Take mine.

GOETZ: You don't see me either; you love me. Heinrich hates me, therefore he can convince me; when my own thoughts come from his mouth, I will be able to believe.

HILDA: If I go away, will you promise to fly with me in a moment?

GOETZ: Yes, if I win my case.

HILDA: You know quite well you have decided to lose it. Farewell, Goetz. [*She goes to him, kisses him, and goes out.*]

GOETZ [*throwing aside the bouquet*]: Quickly, to our work! Do me all the harm you can.

HEINRICH [*looking at him*]: This wasn't how I imagined you.

GOETZ: Courage, Heinrich, the task is easy. Half myself is your accomplice against the other half. Begin, search me to the depth of my being, since it is my being that is on trial.

HEINRICH: Is it true that you want to lose?

GOETZ: Of course not, don't be afraid. Only I prefer despair to uncertainty.

HEINRICH: Well ... [*Pause*] Wait: it is a blank in my memory. I am subject to these absences; it will soon come back. [*He walks up and down in agitation.*] Yet I had taken every precaution; this morning I went over everything in my head ... it is your fault; you aren't at all as you ought to be. You should be crowned with roses, with triumph in your eyes; I would have torn away your crown and overturned your triumph; in the end, you would have fallen on your knees. ... Where is your pride? Where is your insolence? You are half-dead – what pleasure can I find in finishing you off? [*In rage*] Ah! I am not yet wicked enough!

GOETZ [*laughing*]: You are working yourself up, Heinrich. Relax, take your time.

HEINRICH: There isn't a moment to lose. I tell you they are on my heels. [*To* THE DEVIL] Prompt me, prompt me; help me to hate him now I'm with him. [*Plaintively*] He is never there when you need him.

GOETZ: I'm going to prompt you myself. [*Pause*] The lands.

HEINRICH: The lands?

GOETZ: Did I do wrong to give them away?

HEINRICH: Ah! your lands. ... But you didn't give them away; you can only give away what you already have.

GOETZ: Well said! Possession is a friendship between man and objects; but in my hands possessions complained. I gave nothing away. I read a public act of donation, that is all. All the same, priest, if it is true that I didn't give them my lands, it is equally true that the peasants received them. How can you answer that?

HEINRICH: They didn't receive the lands because they weren't able to keep them. When the barons have invaded the domain and installed a young cousin of Conrad's in the castle of Heidenstamm, what will remain of this fantasy?

GOETZ: A fine solution. Neither given, nor received; it is very much more simple. The gold pieces of the Devil change into dead leaves when you try to spend them; my benefits resembled them; when you try to touch them, they turn into corpses. But what about the intention? Eh? If I really meant to do good, neither God nor the Devil can take that away. Attack the intention. Tear to pieces the intention.

HEINRICH: It's not worth the trouble; as you couldn't enjoy your possessions you wanted to raise yourself above other men by pretending to despoil yourself.

GOETZ: Oh voice of brass, proclaim, proclaim my evil thoughts; I no longer know if I listen to you or hear my own voice. Therefore all was nothing but lies and counterfeit? I haven't acted; I merely went through the motions. Ah, priest, you are scratching the itching place. And then? After that? What did the mountebank do? You're very short of breath!

HEINRICH [*infected by the frenzy of* GOETZ]: You gave only to destroy.

GOETZ: You're right! It wasn't enough for me to have murdered the heir ...

HEINRICH [*as before*]: You wanted to grind the inheritance to powder.

GOETZ: I seized the ancient domain of Heidenstamm – raised it above my head ...

HEINRICH [*as before*]: And you dashed it against the ground to smash it in pieces.

GOETZ: I wanted my bounty to be more destructive than my vices.

HEINRICH: And you succeeded; twenty-five thousand dead! In one day of virtue you killed more people than in thirty-five years of malice!

GOETZ: Don't forget that those dead were the poor; those very poor to whom I pretended to offer the possessions of Conrad!

HEINRICH: Yes, by God; you always detested the poor.

GOETZ [*raising his fist*]: Dog! [*He stops and begins to laugh.*] I wanted to strike you; that means you were right. Ha! Ha! So that's where the shoe pinches. Insist! Accuse me of detesting the poor and exploiting their gratitude to enslave them more closely. Before I violated souls by torture, now I violate them through the power of Good. I made a bouquet of faded souls of this village. The poor creatures mouthed at me, and I mouthed back, pretending virtue; they have died as useless martyrs, without knowing why they perished. Listen, priest; I had betrayed everyone, including my own brother, but my appetite for betrayal was not yet fulfilled; so, one night, before the ramparts of Worms, I invented a way to betray Evil, that's the whole story. Only Evil doesn't let itself be betrayed quite so easily; it wasn't Good that jumped out the dice-box; it was the worst of Evil. What does it matter, anyway; monster or saint, I didn't give a damn, I wanted to be inhuman. Say it, Heinrich, say I was mad with shame, and that I wanted to amaze Heaven to escape the scorn of men. Come along! What are you waiting for? Speak! Ah, it's true, you cannot speak any more; I have your voice in my mouth. [*Imitating* HEINRICH] You didn't change your skin, Goetz, you altered your language. You called your hatred of men your generosity, and generosity your rage for destruction. But you remained faithful to yourself; faithful; nothing other than a bastard. [*Resuming his natural voice*] My God, I bear witness that he has spoken true; I, the accused, I acknowledge myself guilty. I have lost my case, Heinrich. Are you content? [*He staggers, and leans against the wall.*]

HEINRICH: No.

GOETZ: You are very difficult.

HEINRICH: Oh, my God, is this my victory? How sad it is.

GOETZ: What will you do when I am dead? You'll miss me horribly.

HEINRICH [*meaning* THE DEVIL]: He gives me plenty to do. I shan't have time to think of you.

GOETZ: You are sure they want to kill me?

HEINRICH: Sure.

GOETZ: The kind people. I shall stretch out my neck, and all will be over; a good riddance for everyone.

HEINRICH: Nothing finishes ever.

GOETZ: Nothing? Ah yes, we still have Hell. Well, it will be a pleasant change.

HEINRICH: It won't be any change for you; you are there already. My companion here – [*meaning* THE DEVIL] – tells me that earth is only illusion; there is Heaven and Hell, that is all. Death is a fool's-trap for our families; for the dead man, it all continues.

GOETZ: Then all will continue for me?

HEINRICH: All. You will have possession of yourself for Eternity. [*Pause*]

GOETZ: How near it seemed – Righteousness – when I was an evildoer. You had only to stretch out an arm. I stretched mine out, and Good changed into a breath of wind. Is it then a vision? Heinrich, Heinrich, is Good possible for men?

HEINRICH: Happy anniversary, Goetz. A year and a day ago, you asked me the same question. And I replied no. It was dark, you laughed as you looked at me, and you said: 'You have the soul of a rat.' And then, you wriggled yourself clear with a throw of the dice. Well, look about you; it is dark – another night like the first one, and who is caught in the rat-trap?

GOETZ [*clowning*]: I am.

HEINRICH: Will you wriggle out again?

GOETZ [*becoming serious*]: No. I shall not wriggle out. [*He walks up and down.*] Lord, if You refuse us the means of doing Good, why have You made us desire it so sharply? If You did not permit that I should become good, why should You have taken from me the desire to be wicked? [*He continues his restless pacing.*] Strange that there should be no way out of this.

HEINRICH: Why do you pretend to talk to Him? You know quite well He never answers.

GOETZ: Then why this silence? He who showed Himself to the prophet's ass, why does He refuse to show Himself to me?

HEINRICH: Because you are unimportant. Torture the weak, or martyrize yourself, kiss the lips of a harlot or a leper, die of privation or excesses; God doesn't give a damn.

GOETZ: Then who is important?

HEINRICH: No one. Man is nothing. Don't look so surprised: you have always known it; you knew it already the night you threw the dice. If you didn't why did you cheat? [GOETZ *tries to speak.*] You cheated, Catherine saw you: you forced your own voice to cover the silence of God. The orders you pretend to receive, you yourself send to yourself.

GOETZ [*reflecting*]: Myself, yes.

HEINRICH [*surprised*]: Yes, indeed. You, yourself.

GOETZ [*as before*]: I alone.

HEINRICH: Yes, I tell you, yes.

GOETZ [*lifting his head*]: I alone, priest, you are right. I alone. I supplicated, I demanded a sign, I sent messages to Heaven, no reply. Heaven ignored my very name. I demanded minute by minute what I could BE in the eyes of God. Now I know the answer; nothing. God does not see me, God does not hear me, God does not know me. You see this emptiness over our heads? That is God. You see this breach in the walls? It is God. You see that hole in the ground? That is God again. The silence is God. The absence is God. God is the loneliness of man. There was no one but myself; I alone decided on Evil; and I alone invented God. It was I who cheated, I who worked miracles, I who accuse myself today, I alone who can absolve myself; I, the man. If God exists, man is nothing; if man exists ... Where are you going?

HEINRICH: I am running away; I have no more to do with you.

GOETZ: Wait, father; I am going to make you laugh.

HEINRICH: Be quiet!

GOETZ: You don't know what I'm going to tell you. [*He looks at* HEINRICH *and then says roughly*] You do know!

HEINRICH [*crying out*]: It's not true! I know nothing, I don't want to know!

GOETZ: Heinrich, I am going to tell you a colossal joke; God does not exist. [HEINRICH *throws himself on* GOETZ *and strikes him. Under the rain of blows* GOETZ *laughs and cries out*] He doesn't exist. Joy, tears of joy. Halleluia. Fool! Don't strike me; I have delivered us. No more Heaven, no more Hell; nothing but earth.

HEINRICH: Ah! Let Him damn me a hundred times, a thousand times, provided He exists. Goetz, men have called us traitors and bastard; and they haven't condemned us. If God doesn't exist, there is no way of escaping men. My God, this man blasphemed, I believe in You, I believe. Our Father which art in Heaven, I would rather be judged by an Infinite Being than judged by my equals.

GOETZ: Who are you talking to? You've just said He was deaf. [HEINRICH *looks at him in silence.*] No way of escaping men. Farewell monsters, farewell saints. Farewell pride. There is nothing left but men.

HEINRICH: Men who won't accept you, bastard.

GOETZ: Bah! I'll manage somehow. [*Pause*] Heinrich, I haven't lost my case: it wasn't brought up for lack of a judge. [*Pause*] I am beginning again.

HEINRICH [*startled*]: Beginning what?

GOETZ: My life.

HEINRICH: It would be much too easy. [*He throws himself on* GOETZ.] You shan't begin again. This is the end; the bolt must be shot today.

GOETZ: Let me go, Heinrich, let me go. Everything is changed, I want to live. [*He struggles in the other man's arms.*]

HEINRICH [*choking him*]: Where is your strength, Goetz, where is your strength? How wonderful that you want to live: you'll sweat your guts out in despair! [GOETZ, *weakened by his fast, tries vainly to shake himself free.*] May your whole future in Hell be contained in your last moment.

GOETZ: Let me go. [*He struggles.*] By heaven, if one of us must die, it had better be you! [*He stabs* HEINRICH.]

HEINRICH: Ha! [*Pause*] I don't want to lose my hatred, I don't want to cease to suffer. [*He falls.*] There will be nothing, nothing, nothing. And tomorrow, you will still see the day. [*He dies.*]

GOETZ: You are dead, and the world is still full; you will not be missed by anyone. [*He takes the flowers and throws them on the corpse.*] The comedy of Good has ended with a murder; very well. I could never have gone back on my tracks. [*He calls*] Hilda! Hilda! [*Night has fallen.*] God is dead.

HILDA: Dead or living, what do I care! I haven't given Him a thought for a very long time. Where is Heinrich?

GOETZ: He has gone.

HILDA: Did you win your case?

GOETZ: There was no trial: I tell you God is dead. [*He takes her in his arms.*] We have no witness now, I alone can see your hair and your brow. How REAL you have become since He no longer exists. Look at me, don't stop looking at me for one moment: the world has been struck blind; if you turned away your head, I should be afraid of annihilation. [*He laughs.*] Alone at last!

[*Lights. Torches approach.*]

HILDA: Here they are. Come.

GOETZ: I will wait for them.

HILDA: They will kill you.

GOETZ: Bah! Who knows? [*Pause*] Let us stay: I need the sight of men.

[*The torches draw nearer.*]

CURTAIN

*

SCENE ELEVEN

The peasants' camp.

KARL, *two peasants, and* THE WITCH. THE WITCH *is rubbing the peasants with a wooden hand.*

NASTI [*entering*]: What are you doing?

THE WITCH: Those I touch with this wooden hand become invulnerable; they can deal blows but receive none!

NASTI: Throw that thing away! [*He strides towards her.*] At once. Throw it away. [THE WITCH *takes refuge behind* KARL.] Karl! Are you in this too?

KARL: Yes. Leave her alone.

NASTI: As long as I command here, the captains will tell no lies to their men.

KARL: Then the men can just die with the captains.

NASTI [*to the peasants*]: Get the hell out of here.

[*They go. Pause.* KARL *crosses to* NASTI.]

KARL: You hesitate, Nasti, you dream, and while you dream, the men desert in hundreds! The army is losing its soldiers as a wounded man loses his blood. You must stop this haemorrhage. We no longer have the right to be dainty of our methods.

NASTI: What do you want me to do?

KARL: Give orders that everyone is to let himself be touched by this pretty child. If they believe themselves invulnerable, they will stay.

NASTI: I was dealing with men, you have changed them into beasts.

KARL: Better have beasts that stand and let themselves be killed than men who run away like rabbits.

NASTI: Prophet of error and abomination!

KARL: Very well. I am a false prophet. But you, what can you be?

NASTI: I didn't want to fight this war ...

KARL: That's very possible, but since you weren't able to prevent it, it must mean God was not on your side.

NASTI: I am not a false prophet, but a man the Lord has betrayed. Do as you please. [KARL *goes out with* THE WITCH.] Yes, indeed, Lord, you have betrayed me, for You allowed me to believe I was Your elect. But how can I reproach You for lying to Your creatures, how can I question Your divine love, I who love my brothers as I do, and lie to them as I am lying now?

[GOETZ *and* HILDA *enter, with three armed peasants.*]

NASTI [*with no surprise*]: So you are here.

A PEASANT [*pointing to* GOETZ]: We were looking for him to slit his throat for him, but he isn't the same man any more. He acknowledges his sins, and says he wants to fight in our ranks. So here he is. We've brought him to you.

NASTI: Leave us. [*The peasants go out.*] You want to fight in our ranks?

GOETZ: Yes.

NASTI: Why?

GOETZ: I need you. [*Pause*] I want to be a man among men.

NASTI: Only that?

GOETZ: I know; it's the most difficult of all. That's why I must begin at the beginning.

NASTI: What is the beginning?

GOETZ: Crime. Men of today are born criminals. I must demand my share in their crimes if I desire my share of their love and their virtue. I wanted love in all its purity; ridiculous nonsense; to love a man is to hate the same enemy; therefore I will embrace your hatred. I wanted to do Good: foolishness: on this earth and at this time, Good and Evil are inseparable; I accept my share of Evil to inherit my share of Good.

NASTI [*looking at him*]: You have changed.

GOETZ: Strangely – I lost someone who was dear to me.

NASTI: Who?

GOETZ: Nobody you know. [*Pause*] I demand to serve under your orders as a simple soldier.

NASTI: I refuse.

GOETZ: Nasti!

NASTI: What do you expect me to do with *one* soldier when I lose fifty every day?

GOETZ: When I came to you, as proud as a rich man, you rejected me, and it was right, for I pretended you needed me. But today I tell you I need you, and if you drive me away you will be unjust. It is unjust to drive away a beggar.

NASTI: I am not driving you away. [*Pause*] For a year and a day, your place has been waiting for you. Take it. You command the army.

GOETZ: No! [*Pause*] I was not born to command. I want to obey.

NASTI: Perfect! Very well, I order you to place yourself at our head. Obey.

GOETZ: Nasti, I am resigned to kill, I shall let myself be killed if I must; but I shall never send another man to die. At last, I know what death is. There is nothing afterwards, Nasti, nothing; we have nothing but our life.

HILDA [*silencing him*]: Goetz! Be quiet!

GOETZ [*to* HILDA]: Yes. [*To* NASTI] Leaders are alone; I want men all around me. Around me, above me, and beside me. Let them hide me from the sky. Nasti, allow me to be a nobody.

NASTI: You are not a nobody. Do you believe a leader is worth more than another man? If you refuse the command, you must go.

HILDA [*to* GOETZ]: Accept.

GOETZ: No. Thirty-six years of loneliness are enough.

HILDA: I shall be with you.

GOETZ: You are myself. We shall be alone together.

HILDA [*in a low voice*]: If you are a soldier among soldiers, will you tell them God is dead?

GOETZ: No.

HILDA: You see.

GOETZ: What do I see?

HILDA: You will never be like other men. Neither better nor

worse: different. And if you ever agree, it will be through misunderstanding.

GOETZ: I killed God because He divided me from other men, and now I see that His death has isolated me even more surely. I shall not allow this huge carcass to poison my human friendship; I shall tell the whole truth, if I am forced to do so.

HILDA: Have you the right to take away their courage?

GOETZ: I will do it little by little. At the end of a year of patience ...

HILDA [*laughing*]: In a year's time, we shall all be dead.

GOETZ: If God is not, why am I alone, I who wished to live with all men?

[*The peasants enter, driving* THE WITCH *before them.*]

THE WITCH: I swear it can't do you any harm. If this hand touches you, you become invulnerable.

THE PEASANTS: We'll believe you if Nasti lets himself be touched.

[THE WITCH *goes to* NASTI.]

NASTI: Go to the devil!

THE WITCH [*whispering*]: I have come from Karl! Let me touch you, or the game is up.

NASTI [*aloud*]: Very well. Do it quickly.

[*She touches him. The peasants applaud.*]

A PEASANT: Touch the monk too.

GOETZ: God's blood!

HILDA [*gently*]: Goetz!

GOETZ: Touch away, my pretty, touch away. [*She touches him.*]

NASTI [*violently*]: Go away! All of you! [*They go.*]

GOETZ: Nasti, has it come to this?

NASTI: Yes.

GOETZ: Then you despise them?

NASTI: I despise only myself. [*Pause*] Do you know of a stranger comedy? I who hate lies, lie to my brothers to give them the courage to be killed in a war I detest.

GOETZ: Hilda, this man is as lonely as I am.

NASTI: Far more lonely. You have always been alone. But I was a hundred thousand, and now I am only myself. Goetz,

I knew neither loneliness nor defeat nor anguish, and I am helpless against them.

[*A* SOLDIER *enters.*]

THE SOLDIER: The captains ask to speak to you.

NASTI: Let them come in. [*To* GOETZ] They have come to tell me confidence is dead, and they have no more authority.

GOETZ [*in a loud voice*]: No. [NASTI *looks at him.*] Suffering, anguish, remorse, are all very fine for me. But if you suffer, the last candle goes out; darkness falls. I will take command of the army.

[*Enter the* CAPTAINS *and* KARL.]

A CAPTAIN: Nasti, you must make an end of this war. My men ...

NASTI: You will speak when I give you leave. [*Pause*] I have news for you which is worth a great victory; we have a general, and he is the most famous captain in Germany.

A CAPTAIN: This monk?

GOETZ: Everything except a monk! [*He throws off his robe and appears dressed as a soldier.*]

THE CAPTAINS: Goetz!

KARL: Goetz! My God ...

A CAPTAIN: Goetz! That changes everything!

ANOTHER CAPTAIN: What does it change, tell me? What does it change? He is a traitor. He's probably drawing you into a fine ambush.

GOETZ: Come here! Nasti has nominated me captain and general. Will you obey my orders?

THE CAPTAIN: I'd rather die.

GOETZ: Then, little brother, die! [*He stabs him.*] As for you others, listen to me! I take up this command against my will, but I shall prove a relentless captain. Believe me, there is one chance of winning this war, and that way I will win it. Proclaim immediately that any soldier attempting to desert will hang. By tonight, I must have a complete statement of what men you have under arms, what weapons and supplies; you will answer for everything with your lives. We shall be sure of victory when your men are more afraid of me than they are of the enemy. [*They try to speak.*] No. Not a word.

Go. Tomorrow you will learn my plans. [*They go.* GOETZ *kicks the body.*] The kingdom of man is beginning. A fine start. Nasti, I told you I would be hangman and butcher. [*He has a moment of weakness.*]

NASTI [*laying a hand on his shoulder*]: Goetz ...

GOETZ: Don't be afraid, I shan't flinch. I shall make them hate me, because I know no other way of loving them. I shall give them their orders, since I have no other way of being obeyed. I shall remain alone with this empty sky above me, since I have no other way of being among men. There is this war to fight, and I will fight it.

CURTAIN

HUIS CLOS

CHARACTERS

GARCIN
VALET
INEZ
ESTELLE

A drawing-room in Second Empire style. A massive bronze group stands on the mantelpiece.

GARCIN [*enters, accompanied by the* ROOM-VALET, and *glances round him*]: Mm! So here we are?

VALET: Yes, Mr Garcin.

GARCIN: And this is what it looks like?

VALET: Yes.

GARCIN: Second Empire furniture, I observe . . . Well, well, I dare say one gets used to it in time..

VALET: Some do. Some don't.

GARCIN: Are all the other rooms like this one?

VALET: How could they be? We cater for all sorts: Chinamen and Indians, for instance. What use would they have for a Second Empire chair?

GARCIN: And what use do you suppose *I* have for one? Do you know who I was? . . . Oh, well, it's no great matter And, to tell the truth, I'd quite a habit of living amongst furniture that I didn't relish, and in false positions. I'd even come to like it. A false position in a Louis-Philippe dining-room – you know the style? – well, that had its points, you know. Bogus in bogus, so to speak.

VALET: And you'll find that living in a Second Empire drawing-room has its points.

GARCIN: Really? . . . Yes, yes, I dare say . . . [*He takes another look round.*] Still, I certainly didn't expect – this! You know what they tell us down there?

VALET: What about?

GARCIN: About [*makes a sweeping gesture*] this – er – residence.

VALET: Really, sir, how could you believe such cock-and-bull stories? Told by people who'd never set foot here. For, of course, if they had . . .

GARCIN: Quite so. [*Both laugh. Abruptly the laugh dies from* GARCIN'S *face.*] But, I say, where are the instruments of torture?

VALET: The what?

GARCIN: The racks and red-hot pincers and all the other paraphernalia?

VALET: Ah, you must have your little joke, sir!

GARCIN: My little joke? Oh, I see. No. I wasn't joking. [*A short silence. He strolls round the room.*] No mirrors, I notice. No windows. Only to be expected. And nothing breakable. [*Bursts out angrily.*] But damn it all, they might have left me my toothbrush!

VALET: That's good! So you haven't yet got over your – what-do-you-call-it? – sense of human dignity? Excuse me smiling.

GARCIN [*thumping ragefully the arm of an armchair*]: I'll ask you to be more polite. I quite realize the position I'm in, but I won't tolerate . . .

VALET: Sorry, sir. No offence meant. But all our guests ask me the same questions. Silly questions, if you'll pardon me saying so. Where's the torture-chamber? That's the first thing they ask, all of them. They don't bother their heads about the bathroom requisites, that I can assure you. But after a bit when they've got their nerve back, they start in about their toothbrushes and what-not. Good heavens, Mr Garcin, can't you use your brains? What, I ask you, would be the point of brushing your teeth?

GARCIN [*more calmly*]: Yes, of course you're right. [*He looks round again.*] And why should one want to see oneself in a looking-glass? But that bronze contraption on the mantelpiece, that's another story. I suppose there will be times when I stare my eyes out at it. Stare my eyes out – see what I mean? . . . All right, let's put our cards on the table. I assure you I'm quite conscious of my position. Shall I tell you what it feels like? A man's drowning, choking, sinking by inches, till only his eyes are just above water. And what does he see? A bronze atrocity by – what's the fellow's name? – Barbedienne. A collector's piece. Like in a nightmare. That's their idea, isn't it? . . . No, I suppose you're under orders not to answer questions; and I won't insist. But don't forget, my man, I've a shrewd notion of what's coming to me, so don't you boast you've caught me off my guard. I'm facing up to the situation, facing up. [*He starts pacing the room again.*] So that's that; no toothbrush. And no bed, either. One never sleeps, I take it?

VALET: That's so.

GARCIN: Just as I expected. *Why* should one sleep? A sort of drowsiness steals on you, tickles you behind the ears, and you feel your eyes closing – but why sleep? You lie down on the sofa and . . . in a flash, sleep flies away. Miles and miles away. So you rub your eyes, get up, and it starts all over again.

VALET: Romantic, that's what you are.

GARCIN: Will you keep quiet, please! . . . I won't make a scene, I shan't be sorry for myself, I'll face up to the situation, as I said just now. Face it fairly and squarely. I won't have it springing at me from behind, before I've time to size it up. And you call that being 'romantic'! . . . So it comes to this; one doesn't need rest. Why bother about sleep if one isn't sleepy? That stands to reason, doesn't it? Wait a bit, there's a snag somewhere; something disagreeable. Why, now, should it be disagreeable? . . . Ah, I see; it's life without a break.

VALET: What do you mean by that?

GARCIN: What do I mean? [*Eyes the* VALET *suspiciously.*] I thought as much. That's why there's something so beastly, so damn' bad-mannered, in the way you stare at me. They're paralysed.

VALET: What are you talking about?

GARCIN: Your eyelids. We move ours up and down. Blinking, we call it. It's like a small black shutter that clicks down, and makes a break. Everything goes black; one's eyes are moistened. You can't imagine how restful, refreshing, it is. Four thousand little rests per hour. Four thousand little respites – just think! . . . So that's the idea. I'm to live without eyelids. Don't act the fool, you know what I mean. No eyelids, no sleep; it follows, doesn't it? I shall never sleep again. But then – how shall I endure my own company? Try to understand. You see, I'm fond of teasing, it's a second nature with me – and I'm used to teasing myself. Plaguing myself, if you prefer; I don't tease nicely. But I can't go on doing that without a break. Down there I had my nights. I slept. I always had good nights. By way of compensation, I suppose. And happy little dreams. There was a green field. Just an ordinary field. I used to stroll in it ... Is it daytime now?

VALET: Can't you see? The lights are on.

GARCIN: Ah yes, I've got it. It's *your* daytime. And outside?

VALET: Outside?

GARCIN: Damn it, you know what I mean. Beyond that wall.

VALET: There's a passage.

GARCIN: And at the end of the passage?

VALET: There's more rooms, more passages and stairs.

GARCIN: And what lies beyond them?

VALET: That's all.

GARCIN: But surely you have a day off sometimes. Where do you go?

VALET: To my uncle's place. He's the head valet here. He has a room on the third floor.

GARCIN: I should have guessed as much. Where's the light-switch?

VALET: There isn't any.

GARCIN: What? Can't one turn off the light?

VALET: Oh, the management can cut off the current, if they want to. But I can't remember their having done so on this floor. We have all the electricity we want.

GARCIN: So one has to live with one's eyes open all the time?

VALET: To *live*, did you say?

GARCIN: Don't let's quibble over words. With one's eyes open. For ever. Always broad daylight in my eyes ... and in my head. [*Short silence.*] And suppose I took that contraption on the mantelpiece and dropped it on the lamp – wouldn't it go out?

VALET: You can't move it. It's too heavy.

GARCIN [*seizing the bronze ornament and trying to lift it*]: You're right. It's too heavy.

[*A short silence follows.*]

VALET: Very well, sir, if you don't need me any more, I'll be off.

GARCIN: What? You're going? [*The* VALET *goes up to the door.*] Wait. [VALET *looks round.*] That's a bell, isn't it? [VALET *nods.*] And if I ring, you're bound to come?

VALET: Well, yes, that's so – in a way. But you can never be sure about that bell. There's something wrong with the wiring, and it doesn't always work.

[GARCIN *goes to the bell-push and presses the button. A bell purrs outside.*]

GARCIN: It's working all right.

VALET [*looking surprised*]: So it is. [*He, too, presses the button.*] But I shouldn't count on it too much if I were you. It's . . . capricious. Well, I really must go now. [GARCIN *makes a gesture to detain him.*] Yes, sir?

GARCIN: No, never mind. [*He goes to the mantelpiece and picks up a paper-knife.*] What's this?

VALET: Can't you see? An ordinary paper-knife.

GARCIN: Are there books here?

VALET: No.

GARCIN: Then what's the use of this? [VALET *shrugs his shoulders.*] Very well. You can go. [VALET *goes out.*]

[GARCIN *is by himself. He goes to the bronze ornament and strokes it reflectively. He sits down: then gets up, goes to the bell-push and presses the button. The bell remains silent. He tries two or three times, without success. Then he tries to open the door, also without success. He calls the* VALET *several times, but gets no result. He beats the door with his fists, still calling. Suddenly he grows calm and sits down again. At the same moment the door opens and* INEZ *enters, followed by the* VALET.]

VALET: Did you call, sir?

GARCIN [*on the point of answering 'Yes' – but then his eyes fall on* INEZ.]: No.

VALET [*turning to* INEZ]: This is your room, madam. [INEZ

says nothing.] If there's any information you require . . . ? [INEZ *still keeps silent, and the* VALET *looks slightly huffed.*] Most of our guests have quite a lot to ask me. But I won't insist. Anyhow, as regards the toothbrush, and the electric bell, and that thing on the mantelshelf, this gentleman can tell you anything you want to know, as well as I could. We've had a little chat, him and me. [VALET *goes out.*] [GARCIN *refrains from looking at* INEZ, *who is inspecting the room. Abruptly she turns to* GARCIN.]

INEZ: Where's Florence? [GARCIN *does not reply.*] Didn't you hear? I asked you about Florence. Where is she?

GARCIN: I haven't an idea.

INEZ: Ah, that's the way it works, is it? Torture by separation. Well, as far as I'm concerned, you won't get anywhere. Florence was a tiresome little fool, and I shan't miss her in the least.

GARCIN: I beg your pardon. Who do you suppose I am?

INEZ: You? Why, the torturer, of course.

GARCIN [*looks startled, then bursts out laughing*]: Well, that's a good one! Too comic for words, I, the torturer! So you came in, had a look at me, and thought I was – er – one of the staff. Of course it's that silly fellow's fault; he should have introduced us. A torturer indeed! I'm Joseph Garcin, journalist and man of letters by profession. And as we're both in the same boat, so to speak, might I ask you, Mrs . . . ?

INEZ [*testily*]: Not 'Mrs'. I'm unmarried.

GARCIN: Right. That's a start anyway. Well, now that we've broken the ice, do you *really* think I look like a torturer . . . ? And, by the way how does one recognize torturers when one sees them? Evidently you've ideas on the subject.

INEZ: They look frightened.

GARCIN: Frightened! But how ridiculous! Of whom should they be frightened? Of their victims?

INEZ: Laugh away, but I know what I'm talking about. I've often watched my face in the glass

GARCIN: In the glass? [*He looks round him.*] How beastly of them! They've removed everything in the least resembling a glass. [*Short silence.*] Anyhow, I can assure you I'm not frightened. Not that I take my position lightly; I realize its gravity only too well. But I'm not afraid.

INEZ [*shrugging her shoulders*]: That's your affair. [*Silence.*] Must you be here all the time, or do you take a stroll outside now and then?

GARCIN: The door's locked.

INEZ: Oh! . . . That's too bad.

GARCIN: I can quite understand that it bores you having me here. And I, too – well, quite frankly, I'd rather be alone. I want to think things out, you know; to set my life in order, and one does that better by oneself. But I'm sure we'll manage to pull along together somehow. I'm no talker, I don't move much; in fact I'm a peaceful sort of fellow. Only, if I may venture on a suggestion, we should make a point of being extremely courteous to each other. That will ease the situation for us both.

INEZ: I'm not polite.

GARCIN: Then I must be polite for two.

[*A longish silence.* GARCIN *is sitting on a sofa, while* INEZ *paces up and down the room.*]

INEZ [*fixing her eyes on him*]: Your mouth!

GARCIN [*as if waking from a dream*]: I beg your pardon.

INEZ: Can't you keep your mouth still? You keep twisting it about all the time. It's grotesque.

GARCIN: So sorry. I wasn't aware of it.

INEZ: That's just what I reproach you with. [GARCIN'S *mouth twitches.*] There you are! You talk about politeness, and you don't even try to control your face. Remember you're not alone; you've no right to inflict the sight of your fear on me.

GARCIN [*getting up and going towards her*]: How about you? Aren't you afraid?

INEZ: What would be the use? There was some point in being afraid *before*; while one still had hope.

GARCIN [*in a low voice*]: There's no more hope – but it's still 'before'. We haven't yet begun to suffer.

INEZ: That's so. [*A short silence.*] Well? What's going to happen?

GARCIN: I don't know. I'm waiting.

[*Silence again.* GARCIN *sits down and* INEZ *resumes her pacing up and down the room.* GARCIN'S *mouth twitches; after a glance at* INEZ *he buries his face in his hands. Enter* ESTELLE *with the* VALET. ESTELLE *looks at* GARCIN, *whose face is still hidden by his hands.*]

ESTELLE [*to* GARCIN]: No! Don't look up. I know what you're hiding with your hands. I know you've no face left. [GARCIN *removes his hands.*] What! [*A short pause. Then, in a tone of surprise.*] But I don't know you!

GARCIN: I'm not the torturer, madam.

ESTELLE: I never thought you were. I . . . I thought someone was trying to play a rather nasty trick on me. [*To the* VALET.] Is anyone else coming?

VALET: No, madam. No one else is coming.

ESTELLE: Oh! Then we're to stay by ourselves, the three of us, this gentleman, this lady, and myself. [*She starts laughing.*]

GARCIN [*angrily*]: There's nothing to laugh about.

ESTELLE [*still laughing*]: It's those sofas. They're so hideous. And just look how they've been arranged. It makes me think of New Year's Day – when I used to visit that boring old aunt of mine, Aunt Mary. Her house is full of horrors like that . . . I suppose each of us has a sofa of his own. Is that one mine? [*To the* VALET.] But you can't expect me to sit on that one. It would be too horrible for words. I'm in pale blue and it's vivid green.

INEZ: Would you prefer mine?

ESTELLE: That claret-coloured one, you mean? That's very sweet of you, but really – no, I don't think it'd be so much better. What's the good of worrying, anyhow? We've got to take what comes to us, and I'll stick to the green one, [*Pauses.*] The only one which might do, at a pinch, is that gentleman's. [*Another pause.*]

INEZ: Did you hear, Mr Garcin?

GARCIN [*with a slight start*]: Oh . . . the sofa, you mean. So sorry. [*He rises.*] Please take it, madam.

ESTELLE: Thanks. [*She takes off her coat and drops it on the sofa. A short silence.*] Well, as we're to live together, I suppose we'd better introduce ourselves. My name's Rigault. Estelle Rigault. [GARCIN *bows and is going to announce his name, but* INEZ *steps in front of him.*]

INEZ: And I'm Inez Serrano. Very pleased to meet you.

GARCIN [*bowing again*]: Joseph Garcin.

VALET: Do you require me any longer?

ESTELLE: No, you can go. I'll ring when I want you.

[*Exit* VALET, *with polite bows to everyone.*]

INEZ: You're very pretty. I wish we'd had some flowers to welcome you with.

ESTELLE: Flowers? Yes, I loved flowers. Only they'd fade so quickly here, wouldn't they? It's so stuffy. Oh, well, the great thing is to keep as cheerful as we can, don't you agree? Of course, you, too, are . . .

INEZ: Yes. Last week. What about you?

ESTELLE: I'm . . . quite recent. Yesterday. As a matter of fact, the ceremony's not quite over. [*Her tone is natural enough, but she seems to be seeing what she describes.*] The wind's blowing my sister's veil all over the place. She's trying her best to cry. Come, dear! Make another effort. That's better. Two tears, two teeny little tears are twinkling under the black veil. Oh dear! What a sight Olga looks this morning! She's holding my sister's arm helping her along. She's not crying, and I don't blame her; tears always mess one's face up, don't they? Olga was my bosom friend, you know.

INEZ: Did you suffer much?

ESTELLE: No. I was only half-conscious, mostly.

INEZ: What was it?

ESTELLE: Pneumonia. [*In the same tone as before.*] It's over now, they're leaving the cemetery. Good-bye. Good-bye. Quite a crowd they are. My husband's stayed at home. Prostrated with grief, poor man. [*To* INEZ.] How about you?

INEZ: The gas-stove.

ESTELLE: And you, Mr Garcin?

GARCIN: Twelve bullets through my chest. [ESTELLE *makes a horrified gesture.*] Sorry! I fear I'm not good company amongst the dead.

ESTELLE: Please, please don't use that word. It's so . . . so crude. In terribly bad taste, really. It doesn't mean much anyhow. Somehow I feel we've never been so much alive as now. If we've absolutely got to mention this . . . this state of things, I suggest we call ourselves – wait! – absentees. Have you been . . . been absent for long?

GARCIN: About a month.

ESTELLE: Where do you come from?

GARCIN: From Rio.

ESTELLE: I'm from Paris. Have you anyone left down there?

GARCIN: Yes, my wife. [*In the same tone as* ESTELLE *has been using.*] She's waiting at the entrance of the barracks. She comes there every day. But they won't let her in. Now she's trying to peep between the bars. She doesn't yet know I'm . . . absent, but she suspects it. Now she's going away. She's wearing her black dress. So much the better, she won't need to change. She isn't crying, but she never did cry, anyhow. It's a bright sunny day and she's like a black shadow creeping down the empty street. Those big tragic eyes of hers – with that martyred look they always had. Oh, how she got on my nerves!

[*A short silence.* GARCIN *sits on the central sofa, and buries his head in his hands.*]

INEZ: Estelle!

ESTELLE: Please, Mr Garcin!

GARCIN: What is it?

ESTELLE: You're sitting on my sofa.

GARCIN: I beg your pardon. [*He gets up.*]

ESTELLE: You looked so . . . so far away. Sorry I disturbed you.

GARCIN: I was setting my life in order. [INEZ *starts laughing.*] You may laugh, but you'd do better to follow my example.

INEZ: No need. My life's in perfect order. It tidied itself up nicely of its own accord. So I needn't bother about it now.

GARCIN: Really? You imagine it's so simple as that. [*He runs his hand over his forehead.*] Whew! How hot it is here! Do you mind if . . .? [*He begins taking off his coat.*]

ESTELLE: How dare you! [*More gently.*] No, please don't. I loathe men in their shirt-sleeves.

GARCIN [*putting on his coat again*]: All right. [*A short pause.*] Of course I used to spend my nights in the newspaper office, and it was a regular Black Hole, so we never kept our coats on. Stiflingly hot it could be. [*Short pause. In the same tone as previously.*] Stifling, that it *is*. It's night now.

ESTELLE: That's so. Olga's undressing; it must be after midnight. How quickly the time passes, on earth!

INEZ: Yes, after midnight. They've sealed up my room. It's dark, pitch dark, and empty.

GARCIN: They've slung their coats on the backs of the chairs and rolled up their shirt-sleeves above the elbow. The air stinks of men and cigar-smoke. [*A short silence.*] I used to like living amongst men in their shirt-sleeves.

ESTELLE [*aggressively*]: Well, in that case our tastes differ. That's all it proves. [*Turning to* INEZ.] What about you? Do you like men in their shirt-sleeves?

INEZ: Oh, I don't care much for men, anyway.

ESTELLE [*looking at the other two with a puzzled air*]: Really I can't imagine why they put us three together. It doesn't make sense.

INEZ [*stifling a laugh*]: What's that you said?

ESTELLE: I'm looking at you two and thinking that we're going to live together . . . It's so absurd. I expected to meet old friends, or relatives.

INEZ: Yes, a charming old friend – with a hole in the middle of his face.

ESTELLE: Yes, him too. He danced the tango so divinely. Like a professional . . . But why, why should we of all people be put together?

GARCIN: A pure fluke, I should say. They lodge folks as they can, in the order of their coming. [*To* INEZ.] Why are you laughing?

INEZ: Because you amuse me, with your 'flukes'. As if they left anything to chance! But I suppose you've got to reassure yourself somehow.

ESTELLE [*hesitantly*]: I wonder now. Don't you think we may have met each other at some time in our lives?

INEZ: Never. I shouldn't have forgotten you.

ESTELLE: Or perhaps we have friends in common. I wonder if you know the Dubois-Seymours?

INEZ: Not likely.

ESTELLE: But *everyone* went to their parties.

INEZ: What's their job?

ESTELLE: Oh, they don't do anything. But they have a lovely house in the country, and hosts of people visit them.

INEZ: I didn't. I was a post-office clerk.

ESTELLE [*recoiling a little*]: Ah, yes . . . Of course, in that case . . . [*A pause.*] And you, Mr Garcin?

GARCIN: We've never met. I always lived in Rio.

ESTELLE: Then you must be right. It's mere chance that has brought us together.

INEZ: Mere chance? Then it's by chance this room is furnished as we see it. It's an accident that the sofa on the right is a livid green, and that one on the left's wine-red. Mere chance? Well, just try to shift the sofas and you'll see the difference quick enough. And that thing on the mantelpiece, do you think it's there by accident? And what about the heat here? How about that? [*A short silence.*] I tell you they've thought it all out. Down to the last detail. Nothing was left to chance. This room was all set for us.

ESTELLE: But really! Everything here's so hideous; all in angles, so uncomfortable. I always loathed angles.

INEZ [*shrugging her shoulders*]: And do you think *I* lived in a Second Empire drawing-room?

ESTELLE: So it was all fixed up beforehand?

INEZ: Yes. And they've put us together deliberately.

ESTELLE: Then it's not mere chance that *you* precisely are sitting opposite *me*? But what can be the idea behind it?

INEZ: Ask me another! I only know they're waiting.

ESTELLE: I never could bear the idea of anyone's expecting something from me. It always made me want to do just the opposite.

INEZ: Well, do it, if you can. You don't even know what they expect.

ESTELLE [*stamping her foot*]: It's outrageous! So something's coming to me from you two? [*She eyes each in turn.*] Something nasty, I suppose. There are some faces that tell me everything at once. Yours don't convey anything.

GARCIN [*turning abruptly towards* INEZ]: Look here! Why are we together? You've given us quite enough hints, you may as well come out with it.

INEZ [*in a surprised tone*]: But I know nothing, absolutely nothing about it. I'm as much in the dark as you are.

GARCIN: We've *got* to know. [*Ponders for a while.*]

INEZ: If only each of us had the guts to tell . . .

GARCIN: Tell what?

INEZ: Estelle!

ESTELLE: Yes?

INEZ: What have you done? I mean, why have they sent you here?

ESTELLE [*quickly*]: That's just it. I haven't a notion, not the foggiest. In fact I'm wondering if there hasn't been some ghastly mistake. [*To* INEZ.] Don't smile. Just think of the number of people who . . . who become absentees every day. There must be thousands and thousands, and probably they're sorted out by – by understrappers, you know what I mean. Stupid employees who don't know their job. So they're bound to make mistakes sometimes . . . Do stop smiling. [*To* GARCIN.] Why don't you speak? If they made a mistake in my case, they may have done the same about you. [*To* INEZ.] And you, too. Anyhow, isn't it better to think we've got here by mistake?

INEZ: Is that all you have to tell us?

ESTELLE: What else should I tell? I've nothing to hide. I lost my parents when I was a kid, and I had my young brother to bring up. We were terribly poor and when an old friend of my people asked me to marry him I said 'Yes'. He was very well off, and quite nice. My brother was a very delicate child and needed all sorts of attention, so really that was the right thing for me to do, don't you agree? My husband was old enough to be my father, but for six years we had a happy married life. Then two years ago I met the man I was fated to love. We knew in the moment we set eyes on each other. He asked me to run away with him, and I refused. Then I got pneumonia and it finished me. That's the whole story. No doubt, by certain standards, I did wrong to sacrifice my youth to a man nearly three times my age. [*To* GARCIN.] Do *you* think that could be called a sin?

GARCIN: Certainly not. [*A short silence.*] And now, tell me, do you think it's a crime to stand by one's principles?

ESTELLE: Of course not. Surely no one could blame a man for that!

GARCIN: Wait a bit! I ran a pacifist newspaper. Then war broke out. What was I to do? Everyone was watching me, wondering 'Will he dare?' Well I dared. I folded my arms and they shot me. Had I done anything wrong?

ESTELLE [*laying her hand on his arm*]: Wrong? On the contrary. You were . . .

INEZ [*breaks in ironically*]: . . . a hero! And how about your wife, Mr Garcin?

GARCIN: That's simple. I'd rescued her from . . . from the gutter.

ESTELLE [*to* INEZ]: You see! You see!

INEZ: Yes, I see. [*A pause.*] Look here! What's the point of play-acting, trying to throw dust in each other's eyes? We're all tarred with the same brush.

ESTELLE [*indignantly*]: How dare you!

INEZ: Yes, we are criminals – murderers – all three of us. We're in hell, my pets, they never make mistakes, and people aren't damned for nothing.

ESTELLE: Stop! For heaven's sake . . .

INEZ: In hell! Damned souls – that's us, all three!

ESTELLE: Keep quiet! I forbid you to use such disgusting words.

INEZ: A damned soul – that's you, my little plaster saint. And ditto our friend there, the noble pacifist. We've had our hour of pleasure, haven't we? There have been people who burnt their lives out for our sakes – and we chuckled over it. So now we have to pay the reckoning.

GARCIN [*raising his fist*]: Will you keep your mouth shut, damn it!

INEZ [*confronting him fearlessly, but with a look of vast surprise*]: Well, well! [*A pause.*] Ah, I understand now. I know why they've put us three together.

GARCIN: I advise you to . . . to think twice before you say any more.

INEZ: Wait! You'll see how simple it is. Childishly simple. Obviously there aren't any physical torments – you agree, don't you? And yet we're in hell. And no one else will come here. We'll stay in this room together, the three of us, for ever and ever . . . In short, there's someone absent here, the official torturer.

GARCIN [*sotto voce*]: I'd noticed that.

INEZ: It's obvious what they're after – an economy of man-power . . . or devil-power, if you prefer. The same idea as in the cafeteria where customers serve themselves.

ESTELLE: What ever do you mean?

INEZ: I mean that each of us will act as torturer of the two others.

[*There is a short silence, while they digest this information.*]

GARCIN [*gently*]: No, I shall never be your torturer. I wish neither of you any harm, and I've no concern with you. None at all. So the solution's easy enough; each of us stays put in his or her corner, and takes no notice of the others. You here, you here, and I there. Like soldiers at our posts. Also, we mustn't speak. Not one word. That won't be difficult; each of us has plenty of material for self-communings. I think I could stay ten thousand years with only my thoughts for company.

ESTELLE: Have *I* got to keep silent, too?

GARCIN: Yes. And that way we . . . we'll work out our salvation. Looking into ourselves, never raising our heads. Agreed?

INEZ: Agreed.

ESTELLE [*after some hesitation*]: I agree.

GARCIN: Then . . . Good-bye.

[*He goes to his sofa, and buries his head in his hands. There is a long silence; then* INEZ *begins singing to herself.*]

INEZ: [*Singing.*]

What a crowd in Whitefriars Lane!
They've set trestles in a row,
With a scaffold and the knife,
And a pail of bran below.
Come, good folks, to Whitefriars Lane,
Come to see the merry show!

The headsman rose at crack of dawn,
He'd a long day's work in hand,
Chopping heads off generals,
Priests and peers and admirals,
All the highest in the land.
What a crowd in Whitefriars Lane!

See them standing in a line,
Ladies all dressed up so fine.
But their heads have got to go,
Head and hats roll down below.
Come, good folks, to Whitefriars Lane
Come to see the merry show!

[*Meanwhile* ESTELLE *has been plying her powder-puff and lipstick. She looks round for a mirror, fumbles in her bag, then turns towards* GARCIN.]

ESTELLE: Excuse me, have you a glass? [GARCIN *does not answer.*] Any sort of glass, a pocket-mirror will do. [GARCIN *remains silent.*] Even if you won't speak to me, you might lend me a glass.

[*His head still buried in his hands,* GARCIN *ignores her.*]

INEZ [*eagerly*]: Don't worry! I've a glass in my bag. [*She opens her bag. Angrily.*] It's gone! They must have taken it from me at the entrance.

ESTELLE: How tiresome!

[*A short silence.* ESTELLE *shuts her eyes and sways, as if about to faint.* INEZ *runs forward and holds her up.*]

INEZ: What's the matter?

ESTELLE [*opens her eyes and smiles*]: I feel so queer. [*She pats herself.*] Don't you ever get taken that way? When I can't see myself I begin to wonder if I really and truly exist. I pat myself just to make sure, but it doesn't help much.

INEZ: You're lucky. I'm always conscious of myself – in my mind. Painfully conscious.

ESTELLE: Ah yes, in your mind. But everything that goes on in one's head is so vague, isn't it? It makes one want to sleep. [*She is silent for a while.*] I've six big mirrors in my bedroom. There they are. I can see them. But they don't see me. They're reflecting the carpet, the settee, the window . . . but how empty it is, a glass in which I'm absent. When I talked to people I always made sure there was one near by in which I could see myself. I watched myself talking. And somehow it kept me alert, seeing myself as the others saw me . . . Oh dear! My lipstick! I'm sure I've put it on all crooked. No, I can't do without a looking-glass for ever and ever, I simply can't.

INEZ: Suppose I try to be your glass? Come and pay me a visit, dear. Here's a place for you on my sofa.

ESTELLE: But – [*Points to* GARCIN.]

INEZ: Oh, he doesn't count.

ESTELLE: But we're going to . . . to hurt each other. You said it yourself.

INEZ: Do I look as if I wanted to hurt you?

ESTELLE: One never can tell.

INEZ: Much more likely *you'll* hurt *me*. Still, what does it matter? If I've got to suffer, it may as well be at your hands, your pretty hands. Sit down. Come closer. Closer. Look into my eyes. What do you see?

ESTELLE: Oh, I'm there! But so tiny I can't see myself properly.

INEZ: But *I* can. Every inch of you. Now ask me questions. I'll be as candid as any looking-glass.

[ESTELLE *seems rather embarrassed and turns to* GARCIN, *as if appealing to him for help.*]

ESTELLE: Please, Mr Garcin. Sure our chatter isn't boring you?

[GARCIN *makes no reply.*]

INEZ: Don't worry about him. As I said, he doesn't count. We're by ourselves . . . Ask away.

ESTELLE: Are my lips all right?

INEZ: Show! No, they're a bit smudgy.

ESTELLE: I thought as much. Luckily [*throws a quick glance at* GARCIN] no one's seen me. I'll try again.

INEZ: That's better. No. Follow the line of your lips. Wait! I'll guide your hand. There. That's quite good.

ESTELLE: As good as when I came in?

INEZ: Far better. Crueller. Your mouth looks quite diabolical that way.

ESTELLE: Good gracious! And you say you like it! How maddening, not being able to see for myself! You're quite sure, Miss Serrano, that it's all right now?

INEZ: Won't you call me Inez?

ESTELLE: Are you sure it looks all right?

INEZ: You're lovely, Estelle.

ESTELLE: But how can I rely upon your taste? Is it the same as my taste? Oh, how sickening it all is, enough to drive one crazy!

INEZ: I *have* your taste, my dear, because I like you so much. Look at me. No, straight. Now smile. I'm not so ugly, either. Aren't I nicer than your glass?

ESTELLE: Oh, I don't know. You scare me rather. My reflection in the glass never did that; of course I knew it so well. Like something I had tamed . . . I'm going to smile and my smile will sink down into your pupils, and heaven knows what it will become.

INEZ: And why shouldn't you 'tame' *me*? [*The women gaze at each other,* ESTELLE *with a sort of fearful fascination.*] Listen! I want you to call me 'Inez'. We must be great friends.

ESTELLE: I don't make friends with women very easily.

INEZ: Not with postal clerks, you mean? Hullo, what's that – that nasty red spot at the bottom of your cheek? A pimple?

ESTELLE: A pimple? Oh, how simply foul! Where?

INEZ: There . . . You know the way they catch larks – with

a mirror? I'm your lark-mirror, my dear, and you can't escape me . . . There isn't any pimple, not a trace of one. So what about it? Suppose the mirror started telling lies? Or suppose I covered my eyes – as he is doing – and refused to look at you, all that loveliness of yours would be wasted on the desert air. No, don't be afraid, I can't help looking at you, I shan't turn my eyes away. And I'll be nice to you, ever so nice. Only you must be nice to me too.

[*A short silence.*]

ESTELLE: Are you really . . . attracted by me?

INEZ: Very much indeed.

[*Another short silence.*]

ESTELLE [*indicating* GARCIN *by a slight movement of her head*]: But I wish he'd notice me, too.

INEZ: Of course! Because he's a Man! [*To* GARCIN.] You've won. [GARCIN *says nothing.*] But look at her, damn it! [*Still no reply from* GARCIN.] Don't pretend. You haven't missed a word of what we've said.

GARCIN: Quite so; not a word. I stuck my fingers in my ears, but your voices thudded in my brain. Silly chatter. Now will you leave me in peace, you two? I'm not interested in you.

INEZ: Not in me, perhaps – but how about this child? Aren't you interested in her? Oh, I saw through your game; you got on your high horse just to impress her.

GARCIN: I asked you to leave me in peace. There's someone talking about me in the newspaper office and I want to listen. And, if it'll make you any happier, let me tell you that I've no use for the 'child', as you call her.

ESTELLE: Thanks.

GARCIN: Oh, I didn't mean it rudely.

ESTELLE: You cad!

[*They confront each other in silence for some moments.*]

GARCIN: So that's that. [*Pause.*] You know I begged you not to speak.

ESTELLE: It's *her* fault; she started. I didn't ask anything of her and she came and offered me her . . . her glass.

INEZ: So you say. But all the time you were making up to him trying every trick to catch his attention.

ESTELLE: Well, why shouldn't I?

GARCIN: You're crazy, both of you. Don't you see where this is leading us? For pity's sake, keep your mouths shut. [*Pause.*] Now let's all sit down again quite quietly; we'll look at the floor and each must try to forget the others are there.

[*A longish silence.* GARCIN *sits down. The women return hesitantly to their places. Suddenly* INEZ *swings round on him.*]

INEZ: To forget about the others? How utterly absurd! I *feel* you there, down to my marrow. Your silence clamours in my ears. You can nail up your mouth, cut your tongue out – but you can't prevent your *being there.* Can you stop your thoughts? I hear them ticking away like a clock, tick-tock, tick-tock, and I'm certain you hear mine. It's all very well skulking on your sofa, but you're everywhere, and every sound comes to me soiled, because you've intercepted it on its way. Why, you've even stolen my face; you know it and I don't! And what about her, about Estelle? You've stolen her from me, too; if she and I were alone, do you suppose she'd treat me as she does? No, take your hands from your face, I won't leave you in peace – that would suit your book too well. You'd go on sitting there, in a sort of trance, like a Yogi, and even if I didn't see her I'd feel it in my bones – that she was making every sound, even the rustle of her dress, for your benefit, throwing you smiles you didn't see . . . Well, I won't stand for that, I prefer to choose my hell; I prefer to look you in the eyes, and fight it out face to face.

GARCIN: Have it your own way. I suppose we were bound to come to this; they knew what they were about, and we're easy game. If they'd put me in a room with men . . . men can keep their mouths shut. But it's no use wanting the impossible. [*He goes to* ESTELLE *and lightly fondles her neck.*]So I attract you, little girl? It seems you were making eyes at me?

ESTELLE: Don't touch me.

GARCIN: Why not? We might, anyhow, be natural . . . Do you know, I used to be mad keen on women? And some were fond of me. So we may as well stop posing, we've nothing to lose. Why trouble about politeness, and decorum and the rest of it? We're between ourselves. And presently we shall be naked as – as new-born babes.

ESTELLE: Oh, let me be!

GARCIN: As new-born babes. Well, I'd warned you, anyhow. I asked so little of you, nothing but peace and a little silence. I'd put my fingers in my ears. Gomez was spouting away as usual, standing in the centre of the room, with all the pressmen listening. In their shirt-sleeves. I tried to hear, but it wasn't too easy. Things on earth move so quickly, you know. Couldn't you have held your tongues? Now it's over, he's stopped talking, and what he thinks of me has gone back into his head. Well, we've got to see it through somehow . . . Naked as we were born. So much the better; I want to know whom I have to deal with.

INEZ: You know already. There's nothing more to learn.

GARCIN: You're wrong. So long as each of us hasn't made a clean breast of it – why they've damned him or her – we know nothing. Nothing that counts. You, young lady, you shall begin. Why? Tell us why. If you are frank, if we bring our spectres into the open, it may save us from disaster. So – out with it! Why?

ESTELLE: I tell you I haven't a notion. They wouldn't tell me why.

GARCIN: That's so. They wouldn't tell me either. But I've a pretty shrewd idea . . . Perhaps you're shy of speaking first? Right. I'll lead off. [*A short silence.*] I'm not a very estimable person.

INEZ: No need to tell us that. We know you were a deserter.

GARCIN: Let that be. It's only a side-issue. I'm here because I treated my wife abominably. That's all. For five years. Naturally, she's suffering still. There she is: the moment I mention her, I see her. It's Gomez who interests me, and it's she I see. Where's Gomez got to? For five years. There! They've given her back my things; she's sitting by the window, with my coat on her knees. The coat with the twelve bullet-holes. The blood's like rust; a brown ring round each hole. It's quite a museum-piece, that coat; scarred with history. And I used to wear it, fancy! . . . Now can't you shed a tear, my love? Surely you'll squeeze one out – at last? No? You can't manage it? . . . Night after night I came home blind drunk; stinking of wine and women. She'd sat up for me, of course. But she never cried, never uttered a word of reproach. Only her eyes spoke. Big, tragic eyes. I don't regret anything. I must pay the price, but I shan't whine . . . It's snowing in the street. Won't you cry, confound you! That woman was a born martyr, you know; a victim by vocation.

INEZ [*almost tenderly*]: Why did you hurt her like that?

GARCIN: It was so easy. A word was enough to make her flinch. Like a sensitive plant. But never, never a reproach. I'm fond of teasing. I watched and waited. But no, not a tear, not a protest. I'd picked her up out of the gutter, you understand . . . Now she's stroking the coat. Her eyes are shut and she's feeling with her fingers for the bullet-holes. What are you after? What do you expect? I tell you I regret nothing. The truth is, she admired me too much. Does that mean anything to you?

INEZ: No. Nobody admired *me*.

GARCIN: So much the better. So much the better for you. I suppose all this strikes you as very vague. Well, here's something you can get your teeth into. I brought a half-caste girl to stay in our house. My wife slept upstairs; she must have heard . . . everything. She was an early riser and, as I and the girl stayed in bed late, she served us our morning coffee.

INEZ: You brute!

GARCIN: Yes, a brute, if you like. But a well-beloved brute. [*A faraway look comes to his eyes.*] No, it's nothing. Only Gomez, and he's not talking about *me* . . . What were you saying? Yes, a brute. Certainly. Else why should I be here? [*To* INEZ.] Your turn.

INEZ: Well, I was what some people down there called 'a damned bitch'. Damned already. So it's no surprise, being here.

GARCIN: Is that all you have to say?

INEZ: No. There was that affair with Florence. A dead men's tale. With three corpses to it. He to start with; then she and I. So there's no one left, I've nothing to worry about; it was a clean sweep. Only that room. I see it now and then. Empty, with the doors locked . . . No, they've just unlocked them. 'To let.' It's to let; there's a notice on the door. That's . . . too ridiculous.

GARCIN: Three: Three deaths, you said?

INEZ: Three.

GARCIN: One man and two women?

INEZ: Yes.

GARCIN: Well, well. [*A pause.*] Did he kill himself?

INEZ: He? No, he hadn't the guts for that. Still, he'd every reason; we led him a dog's life. As a matter of fact he was run over by a tram. A silly sort of end . . . I was living with them; he was my cousin.

GARCIN: Was Florence fair?

INEZ: Fair? [*Glances at* ESTELLE.] You know, I don't regret a thing; still, I'm not so very keen on telling you the story.

GARCIN: That's all right . . . So you got sick of him?

INEZ: Quite gradually. All sorts of little things got on my nerves. For instance, he made a noise when he was drinking – a sort of gurgle. Trifles like that. He was rather pathetic really. Vulnerable. Why are you smiling?

GARCIN: Because I, anyhow, am *not* vulnerable.

INEZ: Don't be too sure . . . I crept inside her skin, she saw the world through my eyes. When she left him, I had her on my hands. We shared a bed-sitting-room at the other end of the town.

GARCIN: And then?

INEZ: Then that tram did its job. I used to remind her every day: 'Yes, my pet, we killed him between us.' [*A pause.*] I'm rather cruel, really.

GARCIN: So am I.

INEZ: No, you're not cruel. It's something else.

GARCIN: What?

INEZ: I'll tell you later. When I say I'm cruel, I mean I can't get on without making people suffer. Like a live coal. A live coal in others' hearts. When I'm alone I flicker out. For six months I flamed away in her heart, till there was nothing but a cinder. One night she got up and turned on the gas while I was asleep. Then she crept back into bed. So now you know.

GARCIN: Well! Well!

INEZ: Yes? What's in your mind.

GARCIN: Nothing. Only that it's not a pretty story.

INEZ: Obviously. But what matter?

GARCIN: As you say, what matter? [*To* ESTELLE.] Your turn. What have you done?

ESTELLE: As I told you, I haven't a notion. I rack my brain, but it's no use.

GARCIN: Right. Then we'll give you a hand. That fellow with the smashed face, who was he?

ESTELLE: Who . . . who do you mean?

INEZ: You know quite well. The man you were so scared of seeing when you came in.

ESTELLE: Oh, him! A friend of mine.

GARCIN: Why were you afraid of him?

ESTELLE: That's my business, Mr Garcin.

INEZ: Did he shoot himself on your account?

ESTELLE: Of course not. How absurd you are!

GARCIN: Then why should you have been so scared? He blew his brains out, didn't he? That's how his face got smashed.

ESTELLE: Don't! Please don't go on.

GARCIN: Because of you. Because of you.

INEZ: He shot himself because of you.

ESTELLE: Leave me alone! It's . . . it's not fair, bullying me like that. I want to go! I want to go!

[*She runs to the door and shakes it.*]

GARCIN: Go, if you can. Personally, I ask for nothing better. Unfortunately the door's locked.

[ESTELLE *presses the bell-push, but the bell does not ring.* INEZ *and* GARCIN *laugh.* ESTELLE *swings round on them, her back to the door.*]

ESTELLE [*in a muffled voice*]: You're hateful, both of you.

INEZ: Hateful? Yes, that's the word. Now get on with it. That fellow who killed himself on your account – you were his mistress, eh?

GARCIN: Of course she was. And he wanted to have her to himself alone. That's so, isn't it?

INEZ: He danced the tango like a professional, but he was poor as a church mouse – that's right, isn't it?

[*A short silence.*]

GARCIN: Was he poor or not? Give a straight answer.

ESTELLE: Yes, he was poor.

GARCIN: And then you had your reputation to keep up. One day he came and implored you to run away with him, and you laughed in his face.

INEZ: That's it. You laughed at him. And so he killed himself.

ESTELLE: Used you to look at Florence in that way?

INEZ: Yes.

[*A short pause, then* ESTELLE *bursts out laughing.*]

ESTELLE: You've got it all wrong, you two. [*She stiffens her shoulders, still leaning against the door, and faces them. Her voice grows shrill, truculent.*] He wanted me to have a baby. So there!

GARCIN: And you didn't want one?

ESTELLE: I certainly didn't. But the baby came, worse luck. I went to Switzerland for five months. No one knew anything. It was a girl. Roger was with me when she was born. It pleased him no end, having a daughter. It didn't please *me*!

GARCIN: And then?

ESTELLE: There was a balcony overlooking the lake. I brought a big stone. He could see what I was up to, and he kept on shouting, 'Estelle, for God's sake, don't!' I hated him then. He saw it all. He was leaning over the balcony and he saw the rings spreading on the water . . .

GARCIN: Yes? And then?

ESTELLE: That's all. I came back to Paris – and he did as he wished.

GARCIN: You mean, he blew his brains out?

ESTELLE: It was absurd of him, really; my husband never suspected anything. [*A pause.*] Oh, how I loathe you! [*She sobs tearlessly.*]

GARCIN: Nothing doing. Tears don't flow in this place.

ESTELLE: I'm a coward. A coward! [*Pause.*] If you knew how I hate you!

INEZ [*taking her in her arms*]: Poor child! [*To* GARCIN.] So the hearing's over. But there's no need to look like a hanging judge.

GARCIN: A hanging judge? [*He glances round him.*] I'd give a lot to be able to see myself in a glass. [*Pause.*] How hot it is! [*Unthinkingly he takes off his coat.*] Oh, sorry! [*He starts putting it on again.*]

ESTELLE: Don't bother. You can stay in your shirt-sleeves. As things are . . .

GARCIN: Just so. [*He drops his coat on the sofa.*] You mustn't be angry with me, Estelle.

ESTELLE: I'm not angry with you.

INEZ: And what about me? Are you angry with me?

ESTELLE: Yes.

[*A short silence.*]

INEZ: Well, Mr Garcin, now you have us in the nude all right. Do you understand things any better for that?

GARCIN: I wonder. Yes, perhaps a trifle better. [*Timidly.*] And now suppose we start trying to help each other?

INEZ: I don't need help.

GARCIN: Inez, they've laid their snare damned cunningly – like a cobweb. If you make any movement, if you raise your hand to fan yourself, Estelle and I feel a little tug. Alone, none of us can save himself or herself; we're linked together inextricably. So you can take your choice. [*A pause.*] Hullo? What's happening?

INEZ: They've let it. The windows are wide open, a man is sitting on my bed. *My* bed, if you please! They've let it, let it! Step in, step in, make yourself at home, you brute! Ah, there's a woman, too. She's going up to him, putting her hands on his shoulders . . . Damn it, why don't they turn the lights on? It's getting dark. Now he's going to kiss her.

But that's my room, *my* room! Pitch dark now. I can't see anything, but I hear them whispering, whispering. Is he going to make love to her on *my* bed? What's that she said? That it's noon and the sun is shining? I must be going blind. [*A pause.*] Blacked out. I can't see or hear a thing. So I'm done with the earth, it seems. No more alibis for me! [*She shudders.*] I feel so empty, desiccated – really dead at last. All of me's here, in this room. [*A pause.*] What were you saying? Something about helping me, wasn't it?

GARCIN: Yes.

INEZ: Helping me to do what?

GARCIN: To defeat their devilish tricks.

INEZ: And what do you expect me to do, in return?

GARCIN: To help *me*. It only needs a little effort, Inez; just a spark of human feeling.

INEZ: Human feeling. That's beyond my range. I'm rotten to the core.

GARCIN: And how about me? [*A pause.*] All the same, suppose we try.

INEZ: It's no use. I'm all dried up. I can't give and I can't receive. How could *I* help you? A dead twig, ready for the burning. [*She falls silent, gazing at* ESTELLE, *who has buried her head in her hands.*] Florence was fair, a natural blonde.

GARCIN: Do you realize that this young woman's fated to be your torturer?

INEZ: Perhaps I've guessed it.

GARCIN: It's through her they'll get you. I, of course, I'm different . . . aloof. I take no notice of her. Suppose you had a try . . .

INEZ: Yes?

GARCIN: It's a trap. They're watching you, to see if you'll fall into it.

INEZ: I know. And you're another trap. Do you think they haven't foreknown every word you say? And of course there's a whole nest of pitfalls that we can't see. Everything here's a booby-trap. But what do I care? I'm a pitfall, too. For her, obviously. And perhaps I'll catch her.

GARCIN: You won't catch anything. We're chasing after

each other, round and round in a vicious circle, like the horses on a roundabout. That's part of their plan, of course . . . Drop it, Inez. Open your hands and let go of everything. Or else you'll bring disaster on all three of us.

INEZ: Do I look the sort of person who lets go? I know what's coming to me. I'm going to burn, and it's to last for ever. Yes, I *know* everything. But do you think I'll let go? I'll catch her, she'll see you through my eyes, as Florence saw that other man. What's the good of trying to enlist my sympathy? I assure you I know everything, and I can't feel sorry even for myself. A trap! Don't I know it, and that I'm in a trap myself, up to the neck, and there's nothing to be done about it. And, if it suits their book, so much the better!

GARCIN [*gripping her shoulders*]: Well, *I*, anyhow, can feel sorry for you, too. Look at me, we're naked, naked right through and I can see into your heart. That's one link between us. Do you think I'd want to hurt you? I don't regret anything, I'm dried up, too. But for you I can still feel pity.

INEZ [*who has let him keep his hands on her shoulders until now, shakes herself loose*]: Don't. I hate being pawed about. And keep your pity for yourself. Don't forget, Garcin, that there are traps for you, too, in this room. All nicely set for you. You'd do better to watch your own interests. [*A pause.*] But, if you will leave us in peace, this child and me, I'll see I don't do you any harm.

GARCIN [*gazes at her for a moment, then shrugs his shoulders*]: Very well.

ESTELLE [*raising her head*]: Please, Garcin.

GARCIN: What do you want of me?

ESTELLE [*rises and goes up to him*]: You can help *me*, anyhow.

GARCIN: If you want help, apply to her.

[INEZ *has come up and is standing behind* ESTELLE, *but without touching her. During the dialogue that follows she speaks almost in her ear. But* ESTELLE *keeps her eyes on* GARCIN, *who observes her without speaking, and she addresses her answers to him, as if it were he who is questioning her.*]

ESTELLE: I implore you, Garcin . . . you gave me your promise, didn't you? Help me quick. I don't want to be left alone. Olga's taken him to a cabaret.

INEZ: Taken whom?

ESTELLE: Peter . . . Oh, now they're dancing together.

INEZ: Who's Peter?

ESTELLE: Such a silly boy. He called me his glancing stream – just fancy! He was terribly in love with me . . . She's persuaded him to come out with her tonight.

INEZ: Do you love him?

ESTELLE: They're sitting down now. She's puffing like a grampus. What a fool the girl is to insist on dancing! But I dare say she does it to reduce . . . No, of course I don't love him; he's only eighteen, and I'm not a baby-snatcher.

INEZ: Then why bother about them? What difference can it make?

ESTELLE: He belonged to me.

INEZ: Nothing on earth belongs to you any more.

ESTELLE: I tell you he was mine. All mine.

INEZ: Yes, he *was* yours – once. But now – Try to make him hear, try to touch him. Olga can touch him, talk to him as much as she likes. That's so, isn't it? She can squeeze his hands, rub herself against him . . .

ESTELLE: Yes, look! She's pressing her great fat chest against him, puffing and blowing in his face. But, my poor little lamb, can't you see how ridiculous she is, why don't you laugh at her? Oh, once I'd have only had to glance at them, and she'd have slunk away. Is there really nothing, nothing left of me?

INEZ: Nothing whatever. Nothing of you's left on earth – not even a shadow. All you own is here. Would you like that paper-knife? Or that ornament on the mantelpiece? That blue sofa's yours. And I, my dear, am yours for ever.

ESTELLE: You mine! That's good! Well, which of you two would dare to call me his glancing stream, his crystal girl? You know too much about me, you know I'm rotten through and through . . . Peter dear, think of me, fix your thoughts on me, and save me. All the time you're thinking 'my glancing stream, my crystal girl', I'm only half here, I'm only half wicked, and half of me is down there with you, clean and bright and crystal-clear as running water . . . Oh, just look at her face, all scarlet, like a tomato! No, it's absurd, we've laughed at her together, you and I, often and often . . . What's that tune, I always loved it? Yes, the St Louis Blues . . . All right, dance away, dance away. Garcin, I wish you could see her, you'd die of laughing. Only – she'll never know I *see* her. Yes, I see you, Olga, with your hair all anyhow, and you do look a dope, my dear. Oh, now you're treading on his toes. It's a scream! Hurry up! Quicker! Quicker! He's dragging her along, bundling her round and round – it's too ghastly! He always said I was so light, he loved to dance with me. [*She is dancing as she speaks.*] I tell you, Olga, I can see you. No, she doesn't care, she's dancing through my gaze. What's that? What's that you said? 'Our poor dear Estelle'? Oh, don't be such a humbug! You didn't even shed a tear at the funeral . . . And she has the nerve to talk to him about her poor dear friend Estelle! How dare she discuss me with Peter? Now then, keep time. She never could dance and talk at once. Oh, what's that . . .? No, no. Don't tell him. Please, please don't tell him. You can keep him, do what you like with him, but please don't tell him about – that! [*She has stopped dancing.*] All right. You can have him now. Isn't it *foul*, Garcin? She's told him everything, about Roger, my trip to Switzerland, the baby. 'Poor Estelle wasn't exactly . . .' No, I wasn't exactly . . . True enough. He's looking grave, shaking his head, but he doesn't seem so very much surprised, not what one'd expect. Keep him then – I won't haggle with you over his long eyelashes, his pretty girlish face. They're yours for the asking. His glancing stream, his crystal. Well, the crystal's shattered into bits. 'Poor Estelle!' Dance, dance, dance. On with it. But do keep time. One, two. One, two. How I'd love to go down to earth for just a moment and dance with him again. [*She dances again for some moments.*] The music's growing fainter. They've turned down the lights, like they do for a tango. Why are they playing so softly? Louder, please. I can't hear. It's so far away, so far away. I . . . I can't hear a sound. [*She stops dancing.*] All over. It's the end. The earth has left me. [*To* GARCIN.] Don't turn from me . . . please. Take me in your arms.

[*Behind* ESTELLE'S *back*, INEZ *signs to* GARCIN *to move away.*]

INEZ [*commandingly*]: Now then, Garcin!

[GARCIN *moves back a step, and, glancing at* ESTELLE, *points to* INEZ.]

GARCIN: It's to her you should say that.

ESTELLE [*clinging to him*]: Don't turn away. You're a man, aren't you, and surely I'm not such a fright as all that! Everyone says I've lovely hair and, after all, a man killed himself on my account. You have to look at something, and there's nothing here to see except the sofas and that awful ornament and the table. Surely I'm better to look at than a lot of stupid furniture. Listen! I've dropped out of their hearts like a little sparrow fallen from its nest. So gather me up, dear, fold me to your heart – and you'll see how nice I can be.

GARCIN [*freeing himself from her, after a short struggle*]: I tell you it's to that lady you should speak.

ESTELLE: To her? But she doesn't count, she's a woman.

INEZ: Oh, I don't count? Is that what you think? But, my poor little fallen nestling, you've been sheltering in my heart for ages, though you didn't realize it. Don't be afraid; I'll keep looking at you for ever and ever, without a flutter of my eyelids, and you'll live in my gaze like a mote in a sunbeam.

ESTELLE: A sunbeam indeed! Don't talk such rubbish! You've tried that trick already, and you should know it doesn't work.

INEZ: Estelle! My glancing stream! My crystal!

ESTELLE: *Your* crystal? It's grotesque. Do you think you can fool me with that sort of talk? Everyone knows by now what I did to my baby. The crystal's shattered, but I don't care. I'm just a hollow dummy, all that's left of me is the outside – but it's not for you.

INEZ: Come to me, Estelle. You shall be whatever you like: a glancing stream, a muddy stream. And deep down in my eyes you'll see yourself just as you want to be.

ESTELLE: Oh, leave me in peace. You haven't any eyes. Oh, damn it, isn't there anything I can do to get rid of you? I've an idea. [*She spits in* INEZ' *face.*] There!

INEZ: Garcin, you shall pay for this.

[*A pause.* GARCIN *shrugs his shoulders and goes to* ESTELLE.]

GARCIN: So it's a man you need?

ESTELLE: Not *any* man. You.

GARCIN: No humbug now. Any man would do your business. As I happen to be here, you want me. Right! [*He grips her shoulders.*] Mind, I'm not your sort at all, really, I'm not a young nincompoop and I don't dance the tango.

ESTELLE: I'll take you as you are. And perhaps I shall change you.

GARCIN: I doubt it. I shan't pay much attention: I've other things to think about.

ESTELLE: What things?

GARCIN: They wouldn't interest you.

ESTELLE: I'll sit on your sofa and wait for you to take some notice of me. I promise not to bother you at all.

INEZ [*with a shrill laugh*]: That's right, fawn on him, like the silly bitch you are. Grovel and cringe! And he hasn't even good looks to commend him!

ESTELLE [*to* GARCIN]: Don't listen to her. She has no eyes, no ears. She's – nothing.

GARCIN: I'll give you what I can. It doesn't amount to much. I shan't love you; I know you too well.

ESTELLE: Do you want me, anyhow?

GARCIN: Yes.

ESTELLE: I ask no more.

GARCIN: In that case . . . [*He bends over her.*]

INEZ: Estelle! Garcin! You must be going crazy. You're not alone. I'm here too.

GARCIN: Of course – but what does it matter?

INEZ: Under my eyes? You couldn't . . . couldn't do it.

ESTELLE: Why not? I often undressed with my maid looking on.

INEZ [*gripping* GARCIN'S *arm*]: Let her alone. Don't paw her with your dirty man's hands.

GARCIN [*thrusting her away roughly*]: Take care. I'm no gentleman and I'd have no compunction about striking a woman.

INEZ: But you promised me; you promised. I'm only asking you to keep your word.

GARCIN: Why should I, considering you were the first to break our agreement?

[INEZ *turns her back on him and retreats to the far end of the room.*]

INEZ: Very well, have it your own way. I'm the weaker party, one against two. But don't forget I'm here, and watching. I shan't take my eyes off you, Garcin; when you're kissing her, you'll feel them boring into you. Yes, have it your own way, make love and get it over. We're in hell; my turn will come.

[*During the following scene she watches them without speaking.*]

GARCIN [*coming back to* ESTELLE *and grasping her shoulders*]: Now then. Your lips. Give me your lips.

[*A pause. He bends to kiss her; then abruptly straightens up.*]

ESTELLE [*indignantly*]: Really! [*A pause.*] Didn't I tell you not to pay any attention to her?

GARCIN: You've got it wrong. [*Short silence.*] It's Gomez; he's back in the press-room. They've shut the windows; it must be winter down there. Six months. Six months since I . . . Well, I warned you I'd be absent-minded sometimes, didn't I? They're shivering, they've kept their coats on. Funny they should feel the cold like that, when I'm feeling so hot. Ah, this time he's talking about me.

ESTELLE: Is it going to last long? [*Short silence.*] You might at least tell me what he's saying.

GARCIN: Nothing. Nothing worth repeating. He's a swine, that's all. [*He listens attentively.*] A god-damned, bloody swine. [*He turns to* ESTELLE.] Let's come back to – to ourselves. Are you going to love me?

ESTELLE [*smiling*]: I wonder now!

GARCIN: Will you trust me?

ESTELLE: What a quaint thing to ask! Considering you'll be under my eyes all the time, and I don't think I've much to fear from Inez, so far as you're concerned.

GARCIN: Obviously. [*A pause. He takes his hands off* ESTELLE'S *shoulders.*] I was thinking of another kind of trust. [*Listens.*] Talk away, talk away, you swine. I'm not there to defend myself. [*To* ESTELLE.] Estelle, you *must* give me your trust.

ESTELLE: Oh, what a nuisance you are! I'm giving you my mouth, my arms, my whole body – and everything could be so simple . . . My trust! I haven't any to give, I'm afraid, and you're making me terribly embarrassed. You must have something pretty ghastly on your conscience to make such a fuss about my trusting you.

GARCIN: They shot me.

ESTELLE: I know. Because you refused to fight. Well, why shouldn't you?

GARCIN: I . . . I didn't exactly refuse. [*In a far-away voice.*] I must say he talks well, he makes out a good case against me, but he never says what I should have done, instead. Should I have gone to the General and said, 'General, I decline to fight'? A mug's game; they'd have promptly locked me up. I wanted to show my colours, my true colours, do you understand? I wasn't going to be silenced. [*To* ESTELLE.] So I . . . I took the train . . . They caught me at the frontier.

ESTELLE: Where were you trying to go?

GARCIN: To Mexico. I meant to launch a pacifist newspaper down there. [*A short silence.*] Well why don't you speak?

ESTELLE: What could I say? You acted quite rightly, as you didn't want to fight. [GARCIN *makes a fretful gesture.*] But, darling, how on earth can I guess what you want me to answer?

INEZ: Can't you guess? Well, *I* can. He wants you to tell him that he bolted like a lion. For 'bolt' he did, and that's what's biting him.

GARCIN: 'Bolted', 'went away' – we won't quarrel over words.

ESTELLE: But you *had* to run away. If you'd stayed they'd have sent you to jail, wouldn't they?

GARCIN: Of course. [*A pause.*] Well, Estelle, am I a coward?

ESTELLE: How can I say? Don't be so unreasonable, darling. I can't put myself in your skin. You must decide that for yourself.

GARCIN [*wearily*]: I can't decide.

ESTELLE: Anyhow, you must remember. You must have had reasons for acting as you did.

GARCIN: I had.

ESTELLE: Well?

GARCIN: But were they the real reasons?

ESTELLE: You've a twisted mind, that's your trouble. Plaguing yourself over such trifles!

GARCIN: I'd thought it all out, and I wanted to make a stand. But was that my real motive?

INEZ: Exactly. That's the question. Was that your real motive? No doubt you argued it out with yourself, you weighed the pros and cons, you found good reasons for acting as you did. But fear and hatred and all the dirty little instincts one keeps dark – they're motives too. So carry on, Mr Garcin, and try to be honest with yourself – for once.

GARCIN: Do I need you to tell me that? Day and night I paced my cell, from the window to the door, from the door to the window. I pried into my heart, I sleuthed myself like a detective. By the end of it I felt as if I'd given my whole life to introspection. But always I harked back to the one thing certain – that I had acted as I did, I'd taken that train to the frontier. But why? Why? Finally I thought: My death will settle it. If I face death courageously, I'll prove I am no coward.

INEZ: And how did you face death?

GARCIN: Miserably. Rottenly. [INEZ *laughs.*] Oh, it was only a physical lapse – that might happen to anyone; I'm not ashamed of it. Only everything's been left in suspense, for ever. [*To* ESTELLE.] Come here, Estelle. Look at me. I want to feel someone looking at me while they're talking about me on earth . . . I like green eyes.

INEZ: Green eyes! Just hark to him! And you, Estelle, do you like cowards?

ESTELLE: If you knew how little I care! Coward or hero, it's all one – provided he kisses well.

GARCIN: There they are, slumped in their chairs, sucking at their cigars. Bored they look. Half-asleep. They're thinking: Garcin's a coward. But only vaguely, dreamily. One's got to think of something. 'That chap Garcin was a coward.' That's what they've decided, those dear friends of mine. In six months' time they'll be saying, 'Cowardly as that skunk Garcin'. You're lucky, you two; no one on earth is giving you another thought. But I – I'm long in dying.

INEZ: What about your wife, Garcin?

GARCIN: Oh, didn't I tell you? She's dead.

INEZ: Dead?

GARCIN: Yes, she died just now. About two months ago.

INEZ: Of grief?

GARCIN: What else should she die of? So all is for the best, you see; the war's over, my wife's dead, and I've carved out my place in history.

[*He gives a choking sob and passes his hand over his face.* ESTELLE *catches his arm.*]

ESTELLE: My poor darling! Look at me. Please look. Touch me. Touch me. [*She takes his hand and puts it on her neck.*] There! Keep your hand there. [GARCIN *makes a fretful movement.*] No, don't move. Why trouble what those men are thinking? They'll die off one by one. Forget them. There's only me, now.

GARCIN: But *they* won't forget *me*, not they! They'll die, but others will come after them to carry on the legend. I've left my fate in their hands.

ESTELLE: You think too much, that's your trouble.

GARCIN: What else is there to do now? I was a man of action once . . . Oh, if only I could be with them again, for just one day – I'd fling their lie in their teeth. But I'm locked out; they're passing judgement on my life without troubling about me, and they're right, because I'm dead. Dead and done with. [*Laughs.*] A back number.

[*A short pause.*]

ESTELLE [*gently*]: Garcin.

GARCIN: Still there? Now listen! I want you to do me a service. No, don't shrink away. I know it must seem strange to you, having someone asking you for help; you're not used to that. But if you'll make the effort, if you'll only *will* it hard enough, I dare say we can really love each other. Look at it this way. A thousand of them are proclaiming I'm a coward; but what do numbers matter? If there's someone, just one person, to say quite positively I did not run away, that I'm not the sort who runs away, that I'm brave and decent and the rest of it – well, that one person's faith would save me. Will you have that faith in me? Then I shall love you and cherish you for ever. Estelle – will you?

ESTELLE [*laughing*]: Oh, you dear silly man, do you think I could love a coward?

GARCIN: But just now you said –

ESTELLE: I was only teasing you. I like men, my dear, who're real men, with tough skin and strong hands. You haven't a coward's chin, or a coward's mouth, or a coward's voice, or a coward's hair. And it's for your mouth, your hair, your voice, I love you.

GARCIN: Do you mean this? *Really* mean it?

ESTELLE: Shall I swear it?

GARCIN: Then I snap my fingers at them all, those below and those in here. Estelle, we shall climb out of hell. [INEZ *gives a shrill laugh. He breaks off and stares at her.*] What's that?

INEZ [*still laughing*]: But she doesn't mean a word of what she says. How can you be such a simpleton? 'Estelle, am I a coward?' As if she cared a damn either way.

ESTELLE: Inez, how dare you? [*To* GARCIN.] Don't listen to her. If you want me to have faith in you, you must begin by trusting me.

INEZ: That's right! That's right! Trust away! She wants a man – that far you can trust her – she wants a man's arm round her waist, a man's smell, a man's eyes glowing with desire. And that's all she wants. She'd assure you you were

God Almighty if she thought it would give you pleasure.

GARCIN: Estelle, is this true? Answer me. Is it true?

ESTELLE: What do you expect me to say? Don't you realize how maddening it is to have to answer questions one can't make head or tail of? [*She stamps her foot.*] You do make things difficult . . . Anyhow, I'd love you just the same, even if you were a coward. Isn't that enough?

[*A short pause.*]

GARCIN [*to the two women*]: You disgust me, both of you. [*He goes towards the door.*]

ESTELLE: What are you up to?

GARCIN: I'm going.

INEZ [*quickly*]: You won't get far. The door is locked.

GARCIN: I'll *make* them open it. [*He presses the bell-push. The bell does not ring.*]

ESTELLE: Please! Please!

INEZ [*to* ESTELLE]: Don't worry, my pet. The bell doesn't work.

GARCIN: I tell you they shall open. [*Drums on the door.*] I can't endure it any longer, I'm through with you both. [ESTELLE *runs to him; he pushes her away.*] Go away. You're even fouler than she. I won't let myself get bogged in your eyes. You're soft and slimy. Ugh! [*Bangs on the door again.*] Like an octopus. Like a quagmire.

ESTELLE: I beg you, oh I beg you not to leave me. I'll promise not to speak again, I won't trouble you in any way – but don't go. I daren't be left alone with Inez, now she's shown her claws.

GARCIN: Look after yourself. I never asked you to come here.

ESTELLE: Oh, how mean you are! Yes, it's quite true you're a coward.

INEZ [*going up to* ESTELLE]: Well, my little sparrow fallen from the nest, I hope you're satisfied now. You spat in my face – playing up to him, of course – and we had a tiff on his account. But he's going, and a good riddance it will be. We two women will have the place to ourselves.

ESTELLE: You won't gain anything. If that door opens, I'm going, too.

INEZ: Where?

ESTELLE: I don't care where. As far from you as I can.

[GARCIN *has been drumming on the door while they talk.*]

GARCIN: Open the door! Open, blast you! I'll endure anything, your red-hot tongs and molten lead, your racks and prongs and garrottes – all your fiendish gadgets, everything that burns and flays and tears – I'll put up with any torture you impose. Anything, anything would be better than this agony of mind, this creeping pain that gnaws and fumbles and caresses one, and never hurts quite enough. [*He grips the door-knob and rattles it.*] Now will you open? [*The door flies open with a jerk, and he nearly falls on the floor.*] Ah! [*A long silence.*]

INEZ: Well, Garcin? . . . You're free to go.

GARCIN [*meditatively*]: Now I wonder why that door opened.

INEZ: What are you waiting for? Hurry up and go.

GARCIN: I shall not go.

INEZ: And you, Estelle? [ESTELLE *does not move.* INEZ *bursts out laughing.*] So what? Which shall it be? Which of the three of us will leave? The barrier's down, why are we waiting? . . . But what a situation! It's a scream! We're . . . inseparables!

[ESTELLE *springs at her from behind.*]

ESTELLE: Inseparables? Garcin, come and lend a hand. Quickly. We'll push her out and slam the door on her. That'll teach her a lesson.

INEZ [*struggling with* ESTELLE]: Estelle! I beg you, let me stay. I won't go, I won't go! Not into the passage.

GARCIN: Let go of her.

ESTELLE: You're crazy. She hates you.

GARCIN: It's because of her I'm staying here.

[ESTELLE *releases* INEZ *and stares dumbfoundedly at* GARCIN.]

INEZ: Because of me? [*Pause.*] All right, shut the door. It's ten times hotter here since it opened. [GARCIN *goes to the door and shuts it.*] Because of me, you said?

GARCIN: Yes. *You*, anyhow, know what it means to be a coward.

INEZ: Yes, I know.

GARCIN: And you know what wickedness is, and shame, and fear. There were days when you peered into yourself, into the secret places of your heart, and what you saw there made you faint with horror. And then, next day, you didn't know what to make of it, you couldn't interpret the horror you had glimpsed the day before. Yes, you know what evil *costs*. And when you say I'm a coward, you know from experience what that means. Is that so?

INEZ: Yes.

GARCIN: So it's you whom I have to convince; you are of my kind. Did you suppose I meant to go? No, I couldn't leave you here, gloating over my defeat, with all those thoughts about me running in your head.

INEZ: Do you really wish to convince me?

GARCIN: That's the one and only thing I wish for now. I can't hear them any longer, you know. Probably that means they're through with me. For good and all. The curtain's down, nothing of me is left on earth – not even the name of coward. So, Inez, we're alone. Only you two remain to give a thought to me. She – she doesn't count. It's you who matter; you who hate me. If you'll have faith in me I'm saved.

INEZ: It won't be easy. Have a look at me. I'm a hard-headed woman.

GARCIN: I'll give you all the time that's needed.

INEZ: Yes, we've lots of time in hand. *All* time.

GARCIN [*putting his hands on her shoulders*]: Listen! Each man has an aim in life, a leading motive; that's so, isn't it? Well, I didn't give a damn for wealth, or for love. I aimed at being a real man. A tough, as they say. I staked everything on the same horse . . . Can one possibly be a coward when one's deliberately courted danger at every turn? And can one judge a life by a single action?

INEZ: Why not? For thirty years you dreamt you were a hero, and condoned a thousand petty lapses – because a hero, of course, can do no wrong. An easy method, obviously. Then a day came when you were up against it, the red light of real danger – and you took the train to Mexico.

GARCIN: I 'dreamt', you say. It was no dream. When I chose the hardest path, I made my choice deliberately. A man is what he wills himself to be.

INEZ: Prove it. Prove it was no dream. It's what one does, and nothing else, that shows the stuff one's made of.

GARCIN: I died too soon. I wasn't allowed time to . . . to do my deeds.

INEZ: One always dies too soon – or too late. And yet one's whole life is complete at that moment, with a line drawn neatly under it, ready for the summing up. You are – your life, and nothing else.

GARCIN: What a poisonous woman you are! With an answer for everything.

INEZ: Now then! Don't lose heart. It shouldn't be so hard, convincing me. Pull yourself together, man, rake up some arguments. [GARCIN *shrugs his shoulders.*] Ah, wasn't I right when I said you were vulnerable? Now you're going to pay the price, and what a price! You're a coward, Garcin, because I wish it. I wish it – do you hear? – I wish it. And yet, just look at me, see how weak I am, a mere breath on the air, a gaze observing you, a formless thought that thinks you. [*He walks towards her, opening his hands.*] Ah, they're open now, those big hands, those coarse, man's hands! But what do you hope to do? You can't throttle thoughts with hands. So you've no choice, you must convince me, and you're at my mercy.

ESTELLE: Garcin!

GARCIN: What?

ESTELLE: Revenge yourself.

GARCIN: How?

ESTELLE: Kiss me, darling – then you'll hear her squeal.

GARCIN: That's true, Inez. I'm at your mercy, but you're at mine as well.

[*He bends over* ESTELLE. INEZ *gives a little cry.*]

INEZ: Oh, you coward, you weakling, running to women to console you!

ESTELLE: That's right, Inez. Squeal away.

INEZ: What a lovely pair you make! If you could see his big

paw splayed out on your back, rucking up your skin and creasing the silk. Be careful, though! He's perspiring, his hand will leave a blue stain on your dress.

ESTELLE: Squeal away, Inez, squeal away! . . . Hug me tight, darling; tighter still – that'll finish her off, and a good thing too!

INEZ: Yes, Garcin, she's right. Carry on with it, press her to you till you feel your bodies melting into each other; a lump of warm, throbbing flesh . . . Love's a grand solace, isn't it, my friend? Deep and dark as sleep. But I'll see you don't sleep.

[GARCIN *makes a slight movement.*]

ESTELLE: Don't listen to her. Press your lips to my mouth. Oh, I'm yours, yours, yours.

INEZ: Well, what are you waiting for? Do as you're told. What a lovely scene: coward Garcin holding baby-killer Estelle in his manly arms! Make your stakes, everyone. Will coward Garcin kiss the lady, or won't he dare? What's the betting? I'm watching you, everybody's watching, I'm a crowd all by myself. Do you hear the crowd? Do you hear them muttering, Garcin? Mumbling and muttering. 'Coward! Coward! Coward! Coward!' – that's what they're saying . . . It's no use trying to escape. I'll never let you go. What do you hope to get from her silly lips? Forgetfulness? But I shan't forget you, not I! 'It's I you must convince.' So come to me, I'm waiting. Come along now . . . Look how obedient he is, like a well trained dog who comes when his mistress calls. You can't hold him, and you never will.

GARCIN: Will night never come?

INEZ: Never.

GARCIN: You will always see me?

INEZ: Always.

[GARCIN *moves away from* ESTELLE *and takes some steps across the room. He goes to the bronze ornament.*]

GARCIN: This bronze. [*Strokes it thoughtfully.*] Yes, now's the moment; I'm looking at this thing on the mantelpiece, and I understand that I'm in hell. I tell you, everything's been thought out beforehand. They knew I'd stand at the fireplace stroking this thing of bronze, with all those eyes intent on me. Devouring me. [*He swings round abruptly.*] What? Only two of you? I thought there were more; many more. [*Laughs.*] So this is hell. I'd never have believed it. You remember all we were told about the torture-chambers, the fire and brimstone, the 'burning marl'. Old wives' tales! There's no need for red-hot pokers. Hell is . . . other people!

ESTELLE: My darling! Please . . .

GARCIN [*thrusting her away*]: No, let me be. She is between us. I cannot love you when she's watching.

ESTELLE: Right! In that case, I'll stop her watching us.

[*She picks up the paper-knife from the table, rushes at* INEZ, *and stabs her several times.*]

INEZ [*struggling and laughing*]: But, you crazy creature, what do you think you're doing? You know quite well I'm dead.

ESTELLE: Dead?

[*She drops the knife. A pause.* INEZ *picks up the knife and jabs herself with it regretfully.*]

INEZ: Dead! Dead! Dead! Knives, poison, ropes – all useless. It has happened *already*, do you understand? Once and for all. So here we are, for ever. [*Laughs.*]

ESTELLE [*with a peal of laughter*]: For ever. My God, how funny! For ever.

GARCIN [*looks at the two women, and joins in the laughter*]: For ever, and ever, and ever.

[*They slump on to their respective sofas. A long silence. Their laughter dies away, and they gaze at each other.*]

GARCIN: Well, well, let's get on with it . . .

CURTAIN